Health and Natural Landscapes: Concepts and Applications

Alan W. Ewert, PhD
Indiana University, USA

Denise S. Mitten, PhD
Prescott College, USA

Jillisa R. Overholt, PhD
Warren Wilson College, USA

Health and Natural Landscapes: Concepts and Applications

Dedication

Much of this book focuses on the positive and beneficial aspects that natural landscapes offer to people across the globe. We acknowledge the large and generous influences that Mother Earth has bestowed on us, both individually and collectively. To this end, we dedicate this book to our mothers, Florence, Lorna, and Linda.

Gulaga Mountain in the background from the Central Tilba area in Australia.
Photo by Lynne Thomas, Yuin-Biripi-Maleema custodian.

CABI is a trading name of CAB International

CABI
Nosworthy Way
Wallingford
Oxfordshire OX10 8DE
UK

CABI
WeWork
One Lincoln Street
24th Floor
Boston, MA 02111
USA

Tel: +44 (0)1491 832111
Fax: +44 (0)1491 833508
E-mail: info@cabi.org
Website: www.cabi.org

Tel: +1 (617)682-9015
E-mail: cabi-nao@cabi.org

A catalogue record for this book is available from the British Library, London, UK.

Library of Congress Cataloging-in-Publication Data

Names: Ewert, Alan W., 1949- author. | Mitten, Denise S., author. |
    Overholt, Jillisa R., author.
Title: Health and natural landscapes : concepts and applications / Alan W. Ewert, PhD, Indiana
    University, USA, Denise S. Mitten, PhD, Prescott College, USA, Jillisa R. Overholt, PhD, Warren,
    Wilson College, USA.
Description: Wallingford, Oxfordshire ; Boston, MA : CAB International, 2021. | Includes bibliographi-
    cal references and index. | Summary: "Natural landscapes are intricately tied to human health and
    well-being, and increasingly valued for their stress-reduction benefits. Providing an overview of the
    history, theory, and individual and societal implications of human connection to landscape, this book
    delivers a research-backed introduction for students, academics and policy makers"-- Provided by
    publisher.
Identifiers: LCCN 2021000949 (print) | LCCN 2021000950 (ebook) | ISBN 9781789245400 (paper-
    back) | ISBN 9781789245417 (ebook) | ISBN 9781789245424 (epub)
Subjects: LCSH: Environmental health. | Natural landscaping--Health aspects.
Classification: LCC RA566 .E948 2021 (print) | LCC RA566 (ebook) | DDC 613/.1--dc23
LC record available at https://lccn.loc.gov/2021000949
LC ebook record available at https://lccn.loc.gov/2021000950

References to Internet websites (URLs) were accurate at the time of writing.

ISBN-13: 9781789245400 (paperback)
        9781789245417 (ePDF)
        9781789245424 (ePub)

DOI: 10.1079/9781789245400.0000

Commissioning Editor: Alexandra Lainsbury
Editorial Assistant: Lauren Davies
Production Editor: James Bishop

Typeset by SPi, Pondicherry, India
Printed and bound in the UK by CPI Group (UK) Ltd, Croydon, CR0 4YY

Contents

Author Biographies

Alan W. Ewert, PhD
Indiana University, USA
aewert@indiana.edu
Alan W. Ewert is a professor emeritus at Indiana University and currently serves on the Board of Directors for Northwest Outward Bound. Prior to this he served as a professor in the Department of Recreation, Park and Tourism Studies and as department chair in the Department of Environmental Health at Indiana University, USA.

Denise S. Mitten, PhD
Prescott College, USA
dmitten@prescott.edu
Denise S. Mitten works with graduate students in the Outdoor Education Leadership MA and Sustainability Education PhD programs at Prescott College. A widely experienced nature and adventure guide, from scuba diving to mountaineering, Professor Mitten developed an award-winning leadership training and apprenticing program for women, programs to strengthen bonding between parents and children, and a leadership program for women felons.

Jillisa R. Overholt, PhD
Warren Wilson College, USA
joverholt@warren-wilson.edu
Jillisa R. Overholt is a professor and chair of the Outdoor Leadership Studies Department at Warren Wilson College in Asheville, North Carolina, USA. She has served as an Outward Bound instructor, environmental educator, camp professional, and Peace Corps volunteer. In her spare time, she enjoys hiking, cycling, and playing outside with her daughter.

Guest Contributors

Tanya Ginwala, MA (ClinPsych)
Adventure Therapy International Committee, India
tanya.ginwala@gmail.com
Tanya Ginwala, MA (ClinPsych) is a psychologist in Dharamshala (India), specializing in adventure and nature-based therapy. Previously with Adventures Beyond Barriers, she is passionate about making nature and adventure experiences accessible and inclusive for all. Tanya is currently the India representative at the Adventure Therapy International Committee, a 33-country consortium that plans the International Adventure Therapy Conference.

Dr. Tonia Gray
Western Sydney University, Australia
t.gray@uws.edu.au
Dr. Tonia Gray is a professor at Western Sydney University, Australia, and her scholarship builds knowledge about connection with nature in educational settings for health and well-being. As a researcher, practitioner, and teacher–educator for over three decades, her participatory research with children and adolescence centers on well-being and human–nature connection, sustainability education, leadership and gender studies, and curriculum development and design.

Gulaga (Mother Mountain)
New South Wales, Australia
Gulaga (Mother Mountain) is nestled on the south coast of New South Wales. High in the misty slopes of my womanly shape I come from the creation of the Dreamtime where I guard the teaching rocks of knowledge sculptured by the wind, rain, heat, and snow. I am the mother of the Yuin people and the teacher of the landscape as far as your eyes can see … I am Gulaga.

Dr. Aya Hayashi
Biwako Seikei Sport College, Japan
ayahayashi@msn.com
Dr. Aya Hayashi is a professor at the Biwako Seikei Sport College, Japan. For her, natural environments like mountains are the place to charge the energy for healthy life, hang out with friends and family, teach students, and conduct research projects.

Dr. Susan Houge Mackenzie
University of Otago, New Zealand
susan.hougemackenzie@otago.ac.nz
Dr. Susan Houge Mackenzie is an associate professor in the University of Otago Department of Tourism, New Zealand, where she investigates links between adventure and psychological well-being. She is a former adventure guide and has provided consulting for government and tourism agencies including New Zealand Riverboarding,

the History Channel, and the United States Forest Service. She is a member of the Adventure Tourism Research Association steering committee.

Nandini Kumar

Hanifl Centre for Outdoor Education and Environmental Study Woodstock School (Mussoorie), India
kumar.nandini04@gmail.com

Nandini Kumar hails from the Himalayan state of Uttarakhand in North India. She is a writer and poet as well as a lover of the outdoors, working at the Hanifl Centre for Outdoor Education and Environmental Study, Woodstock School, Mussoorie. A post-graduate in psychology, she has been writing about the mesmerizing lives of Himalayan people and one of her books (fiction) has won her the Amazon Pen to Publish Award 2018. She has also assisted the Mussoorie Mountain Festival, which is one of the main festivals in India that celebrates various aspects of Himalaya. Her stories have appeared on radio and audible shows and in national magazines.

Lia Naor

University of Haifa, Israel
liawaysofknowing@gmail.com

Dr. Lia Naor is a nature therapist, researcher, and lecturer who trained and teaches nature-based therapy in Israel. Her research focuses on the process of positive change and personal transformation occurring in nature. Her dissertation provides a tentative working model for nature-based therapy.

Lynne Thomas

Aboriginal Education Officer with Narooma Primary School, Australia
lynnethomas27@gmail.com

Lynne Thomas is a proud Yuin/Biripi/Ngarigo woman who lives on the south coast of New South Wales, Australia. Lynne's pastime is sharing knowledge through guided walks into aboriginal special sites, reinforcing cultural heritage, sustainability, and edu-cational programs in the outdoors and Mother Earth, taught to her by her father Guboo Ted Thomas Yuin Tribal Elder (1909–2003), her mother Anne Thomas, and woman elders of the past.

Dr. Guan-Jang Wu

National Taiwan Sport University, Taiwan
guan@ntsu.edu.tw

Dr. Guan-Jang Wu, a native of Taiwan, received his PhD in leisure behavior from Indiana University and has been a faculty member of the National Taiwan Sport University since 2006. His professional experiences include working with NOLS, Outward Bound, and the Wilderness Education Association.

Haoai Zhao

Indiana University, USA
haoazhao@iu.edu

Haoai Zhao is a research assistant and doctoral student from the Department of Health and Wellness Design, School of Public Health, Indiana University. Her research interests focus on studying customer experience and developing scales for measur-ing travel impacts on travelers' mental health.

Preface

Reconnection to the natural world is fundamental to human health, well-being, spirit, and survival.
~Richard Louv, journalist and co-founder of Children & Nature Network

The year 2020 proved to be one of the most challenging and disruptive years in recent history. This disruption had a global reach and was influenced by a spectrum of factors, including political and civil unrest, severe weather patterns, intensifying effects of climate change, faltering economies, and explosive wildfire seasons. But perhaps the most destructive event that year was the rapid growth of the coronavirus disease 2019 (COVID-19) pandemic. One response to that threat now practiced by millions of people across the globe has been to escape to the outdoors as a way to avoid contracting the virus. For many, natural landscapes represent places that are safe from both the virus and many of the other threats posed in large urban settings, while also being locations that facilitate stress reduction and promote well-being. In one sense, this action alone represents the underlying intent of this book: to explore and better understand the relationship between human health and natural landscapes.

Whether a local green space, city park, a small copse of trees or other vegetation, a meandering waterway, a larger state or provincial park, or a wilderness-type area, these landscapes can provide humans with a broad spectrum of physical, psychological, spiritual, and emotional benefits that most of us seek. Many of these outcomes have been measured, while some remain inestimable. While benefits from experiencing natural landscapes such as appreciating the aesthetic beauty of a seascape, walking along a forested trail with a friend, or enjoying a chance for solitude along a babbling stream may be difficult to measure, they can exert a profound influence on us, individually and collectively.

Increasingly, many societies are placing greater value on the health benefits that can be accrued through exposure to natural landscapes. For example, a growing number of physicians now prescribe short visits to local parks or other open spaces as alternatives to the commonly used pharmacological solutions to various health issues. In other cases, the restrictions imposed by the pandemic have allowed citizens to explore their own local natural landscapes, finding places for solitude, family engagement, or simply a chance to see nature. Attributes of natural landscapes that often have strong connections to health include higher air and water quality, reduced noise levels, and modified temperatures. These attributes, combined with the presence of vegetation, aesthetic scenery, and opportunities for physical activity or socialization, can provide salutogenic outcomes such as stress reduction, attention restoration, or improved immune-system functioning. It seems clear that contact with natural landscapes can provide individuals with an antidote to many of the often unhealthy aspects of urban life.

This book explores these positive outcomes by delving into how humans perceive and respond to the natural world. We look at the different stages of human development and how societal perspectives regarding natural landscapes have changed over time. These perspectives influence our responses to current issues such as climate change and pandemics. Examining our worldviews is critical to developing a deeper understanding of human beliefs and relationships with natural landscapes. Moreover, empirically based theories and models can be useful in enhancing that understanding, but other realities are also important such as traditional ecological knowledge (TEK) and a rekindling of a sense of connection with nature. Whether empirically derived in recent decades or handed down through the generations, this knowledge can be useful as we consider the many forms of human well-being, including physical, mental, spiritual, and social.

To be effective, knowledge must be put into practice. In this book, we discuss a variety of applications and consider ways that society can incorporate natural landscapes to enhance human health. Ranging from organized camping and experiential programming to the development of pocket parks, there is a broad and growing spectrum of actions humans can implement to be in relationship with natural landscapes to strengthen their sense of well-being and health. Although much of our discussion focuses on what has been and what is, we also look at the question of what will be. Toward this end, our discussion emphasizes the role that natural landscapes should play in the future. Circling back to our earlier examination of the development of worldviews concerning natural landscapes, we consider the question of how to develop a land ethic for health using natural landscapes for the future. We conclude this book's role in that ongoing discussion regarding health and natural landscapes in the future by providing a set of guiding principles for the reader's consideration. For certainly, just as our health can be influenced by natural landscapes, the health of these natural areas is determined by our own individual and collective actions.

Alan W. Ewert
Denise S. Mitten
Jillisa R. Overholt

Acknowledgments

The authors would like to extend their appreciation to Alexandra Lainsbury from CABI for her insight, follow-through, and assistance during the process of publishing this book, James Bishop, CABI production editor, as well as to Priscilla Sharland for her editing guidance. In addition, we would like to thank Pam Firth for her assistance in the editing process, and Amy Fischer and Stuart Slay for their assistance in preparing and designing the diagrams. Thank you to Lydia Holt Lieb for the cover photo taken on the Wonderland Trail in Mt. Rainier National Park, USA, Lia Naor and Lynne Thomas for the use of their photos from Israel and Australia respectively, and to Walter Holt for his photo guidance and work. Finally, we would like to thank the guest contributors for their insightful perspectives and for highlighting some of the landscape and human interactions in their respective countries.

Mountains and rolling hills from the Central Tilba area in Australia.
Photo by Lynne Thomas, Yuin-Biripi-Maleema custodian.

1 Natural Landscapes and Human Health: an Introduction and Overview

Action on behalf of life transforms. Because the relationship between self and the world is reciprocal, it is not a question of first getting enlightened or saved and then acting. As we work to heal the earth, the earth heals us.

~Joanna Macy, PhD, environmental activist, eco-philosopher, and scholar of systems theory

The importance of environment has long been tied to our overall health and well-being. Natural landscapes, those places and spaces that include natural elements such as plants, trees, water, sunlight, and fresh air, are particularly influential. As a species, humankind evolved in natural landscapes, but in recent centuries, many people have physically isolated themselves from these environments through the work opportunities and comforts of urbanization. Now we find ourselves increasingly embracing natural landscapes as places to restore our health, build resilience and coping strategies, find respite from our heavily built environments, reaffirm our social support systems, and heal the earth.

In the West, it has only been in the last hundred years or so that most humans have lived and worked primarily indoors. During this time, in Western society we have often embraced the value of individualism, focusing mainly on therapies and drugs (many based on compounds in nature) to cure our ills and neglecting the importance of our daily environments. Gallagher (1993) argued that we are organisms, dependent on biology and environmental interactions for our survival, and yet we have built a society that has allowed us to largely obscure these connections and "forget" the many ways that climate, season, sunlight, and other environmental factors influence our day-to-day functioning.

Defining Terms and Concepts

A **landscape** is "part of the Earth's surface that can be viewed at one time from one place and consists of the geographic features that mark, or are characteristic of, a particular area" (National Geographic, n.d.). This term is subdivided into two categories: "**natural landscape**," which is a collection of landforms and vegetative features, and "**cultural landscape**," which is simply any landscape that bears human influence. Following this definition, many of the relatively natural spaces we think of as the natural world—parks, gardens, trails, and so on—are actually cultural landscapes. These are areas that have been defined and maintained via cultural practices, though the level of human intervention varies. We argue that all landscapes have been influenced or modified in some way by humans, and that the distinction between natural and cultural often serves to perpetuate a false human–nature dichotomy. As such, for this book, we use interchangeably the terms landscape and natural landscape to refer to the collection of elements of the relatively natural world as they make up our surroundings, and we consider their influence to human health and well-being. Research suggests that the presence of natural elements in a space is positively impactful to our overall well-being and even heavily urbanized

DOI: 10.1079/9781789245400.0001

landscapes may offer these elements through rooftop gardens, pocket parks, potted plants, and the like. Thus, considering the entire landscape provides the most inclusive approach to understanding human health in relationship to our surroundings.

Urban areas comprise built structures and the external spaces between them; when those external spaces are predominantly "unsealed, permeable, soft surfaces such as soil, grass, shrubs, and trees" (Swanwick *et al.*, 2003), they are referred to as **green space**. This contrasts with **grey space** or sealed, impermeable, or hard surfaces such as concrete or pavement. **Blue space** includes rivers, lakes, coastal areas, and other bodies of water. While historically central to conceptions of healing in the form of spas, baths, and so on, blue spaces have re-emerged in contemporary research in terms of their benefit to public health (Foley and Kistemann, 2015). McDougall *et al.* (2020) completed a review especially focusing on freshwater landscapes, offering that 50% of the world population lives within 3 km of a body of fresh water.

There is a substantial and growing literature that details positive human health effects, psychological and physiological, of exposure to nature, including green and blue space, with evidence suggesting that diversity of species or environments may have specific positive human health benefits. In this book, we use interchangeably the terms green space, **urban green space**, and **urban green and blue space** (**UGBS**) to refer to the integration of natural elements in urban environments to create livable landscapes. This integration can be a key element in the livability of cities, especially as urban densification continues to increase in many countries around the world.

Choosing and identifying terms such as nature, natural environment, and landscape can be challenging due to cultural and societal influences on their meaning. Definitions of these terms often serve to separate humans from natural landscapes in the endeavor to identify what is natural and what is human or cultural. This distinction is rooted in the human–nature dualism inherent to Western culture (Cronon, 1996; King, 2017) and is increasingly being questioned as Westerners begin to recognize themselves as part of the natural world. **Natural environments** have previously been defined as settings that are relatively unchanged or undisturbed by human intervention (Johnson *et al.*, 1997). In the developed world, this definition largely limits natural environments to wilderness areas and other protected or undeveloped spaces. Other authors, however, include less remote settings, such as parks, forested areas, waterside locations, and gardens, many of which are within or close to urban environments and feature varying degrees of human intervention (Mantler and Logan, 2015). Conceptualizing the natural environment is a complex endeavor, and the roles of individual experience, cultural influence, and contextual meaning must all be considered. Nature experience is thus both a subjective phenomenon and a social construction, and yet there is growing consensus that human contact with nature is beneficial to health (Hartig *et al.*, 2014).

This is not simply a philosophical debate, as the way we define terms such as nature and culture impacts broader issues of sustainability, conservation, and the myriad ways humans interact with their environments more broadly (Kimmerer, 2015; King, 2017). Sorvig (2002) suggested that non-European cultures offer a useful approach to defining terms, such as nature and culture, in a less absolute and more approximate manner. The Westernized equivalent to this is the "working" or "operational" definitions, which are "intellectually imperfect, but suited to a particular applied task" (Sorvig, 2002, p. 4). While both terms are limited, they are useful in their ability to help us conceive the differences between humans and the "more-than-human world." In this vein, we sometimes use descriptors such as nature and natural, as in "natural landscape," to signify the predominantly natural and non-built, while recognizing the wide scale of potential human impact ranging from minimal (e.g. wilderness areas) to extensive (e.g. formal gardens or potted plants). While our primary focus is health promotion, this book endeavors to consider the impact of landscapes on human health from a variety of perspectives, including the negative influences of human impacts on the non-human world, including climate change.

Like landscapes, the idea of health has also been conceptualized in a number of ways. In its founding documents, the World Health Organization (WHO, 2020) described health as "a state of complete physical, mental, and social well-being and not merely the absence of disease or infirmity" (p. 1). Since the establishment of the WHO in 1946, the health needs of people around the world have shifted, but the acuity of this definition has remained and is embedded in a commitment to health as a fundamental right and as foundational to peace, security, and global cooperation. **Well-being,** the WHO's foundational concept of health, is often seen as spanning six dimensions of a person's existence—emotional, environmental, intellectual, physical, social, and spiritual—and involving both the micro (immediate, personal) and macro (global, planetary) environments (Blonna, 2012). **Environment,** including the natural, physical, and societal surroundings that affect individuals' functioning, is increasingly being recognized in terms of its role in health outcomes.

Social determinants of health (SDOH) refers to "the conditions in which people are born, grow, live, work and age" (WHO, n.d., para. 1). These conditions directly influence an individual's opportunity to be healthy, are inequitably distributed, and can be changed through policy and governance. SDOH include social and environmental factors such as racism and discrimination, access to nutritious food, exposure to pollution, and access to healthcare and social support networks, and address the interconnectedness between factors such as individual-, interpersonal-, organizational-, community-, and policy-level initiatives. The US Centers for Disease Control and Prevention groups SDOH into five domains: (i) economic stability; (ii) educational access and quality; (iii) healthcare access and quality; (iv) neighborhood and built environment; and (v) social and community context. Emphasizing social determinants, rather than individual factors of well-being, contextualizes disparities and implicates the role of public health organizations and institutions in shaping preventive health strategies. In other words, healthy environments are essential for healthy people.

Quality of life (QoL), a related concept, is a person's ability to enjoy normal life activities and experience an overall sense of well-being. QoL often has a strong connection to individual health perceptions and life functioning. Natural landscapes can aid in improving lifestyle-related diseases and are sometimes thought of as spaces for **healing**—a process that leads to a sense of well-being and impacts the whole person (Mitten, 2004). An indicator of healing is when a person can be in awe of the wonder and beauty of life and of the natural world. While time in natural landscapes may not cure an illness (eradicate a disease, condition, or symptom(s) that the patient has), it can provide healing.

In a **socioecological approach,** health is understood to result from an interwoven relationship between people and their environment. Experiences in landscapes can play a key role in a socioecological approach to health because these environments encourage and enable people to relate to each other and the natural world (Maller *et al.*, 2006). One of the five overarching goals of the Healthy People 2030 Framework is to "create neighborhoods and environments that promote health and safety" (United States Department of Health and Human Services, n.d., para. 1). This includes ensuring access to quality green spaces, designing infrastructure for safe walking and biking, reducing environmental pollution, and providing opportunities for community building. Regular access to healthy natural landscapes facilitates **connectedness to nature** or an individual's sense of positive relationship to the natural world. The prioritization of healthy natural landscapes benefits the health of the entire planet, ultimately helping to solve pressing health and environmental issues.

Foundations

Beliefs that natural spaces can be influential and beneficial for human health date back to over 60,000 years ago (see Chapter 2, this volume). Ongoing research consistently reports that humans generally respond positively to natural settings and usually more positively than they do to built settings or urban ones. For example, natural settings may increase brain activity in regions associated with positive mental outlook and emotional stability, whereas urbanized settings, especially ones with low coherence, may increase activity in the amygdala, a region of the brain associated with threat, arousal, and risk-taking behavior (Kim *et al.*, 2011).

A broadening corpus of research and scholarship supports the primary assumption made in this book that there is a link between landscapes and health-promoting experiences and behaviors for individuals and groups (e.g. Ewert *et al.*, 2014; Franco *et al.*, 2017). For example, time spent in natural environments is important to healthy child development (Charles and Louv, 2020), is linked to educational outcomes (Kuo *et al.*, 2018), can support preventive healthcare (Razani *et al.*, 2020), and can provide effective forms of therapy (Harper and Dobud, 2021). Still, nature can be harsh, and some interactions can result in negative outcomes (Andrews and Gatersleben, 2010; Bruni *et al.*, 2012). Some environments, because of their geographic location and specific conditions such as toxic chemicals from human activities, weather, and topography, present challenges for humans. Additionally, we recognize that people of color and socially and economically disadvantaged people tend to live in areas with higher pollution and have poorer healthcare, making them more susceptible to negative interactions with the environment, including more toxic exposures and less access to green space (Bullard and Wright, 2012; Taylor, 2014).

The second primary assumption made in this book is that the effects of landscapes on human health can be felt, observed, and/or measured. Lariviere *et al.* (2012) suggested that while nature-based experiences often result in positive anecdotal accounts, a substantial amount of variation exists in the quality, perspective, and approach of existing studies. Recent advances in technology have enabled researchers to begin to conduct large-scale epidemiological studies and collect new kinds of data, including physiological biomarkers and brain imagery, to help verify earlier studies (Hartig *et al.*, 2014). Researchers generally agree that contact with nature produces health benefits, but questions of causality, dosage, and long-term outcomes remain. Understanding these potential and real outcomes is made even more urgent by authors such as Williams (2017) and Pergams and Zaradic (2008) who believe that members of industrialized societies are becoming more alienated and physically separated from landscapes and more accustomed to indoor and technology-oriented environments. They argue that this separation from nature has adverse effects on an individual's health and well-being.

The third primary assumption is that for landscapes to beneficially impact human health, we must care for the environment. A number of global issues, including climate change, environmental toxicity, availability of food and water resources, air quality, and pollution, have direct bearing on human health and overall QoL. With an understanding of our need for nature and the opportunity to build connections with surrounding landscapes, people are more likely to be advocates to ensure ecological quality. When people have a deeper understanding of the human–nature connection, and feel that on a visceral level, they often develop a strong ecological conscience leading to positive action.

The Importance of This Book

There are myriad ways that people and landscapes meet, whether for essential resources such as water, minerals, animals, and plants, or simply for the enjoyment of interacting with the natural world. As you read this book, literally millions of people around the globe are connecting with natural landscapes, whether for work or subsistence, for recreation or leisure, or simply as places to be with family and friends. For some, this may take the form of tending a garden or foraging for medicinal plants. For others, it may involve a quiet walk down a winding path, along a wind-swept coastline, or at a nearby municipal park. Still others might engage with the landscape through adventure recreation activities, such as whitewater rafting or mountain climbing.

While precise data on people interacting with landscapes for health-related purposes are limited, inference can be drawn from outdoor recreation statistics. For example, in the USA, over 145 million people or 48.8% of the population participated in some form of recreation in the outdoors in 2017 (Outdoor Foundation, 2018). In Canada, over 73% of the population reported participation in outdoor activities in 2017 (Statistics Canada, n.d.). Similarly, in England in 2014, over 59.3% of the adult population engaged in some form of outdoor activity (Sport England, 2015). In 2018, US national parks received over 330 million visitors, and US state parks received over 807 million visitors (National Association of State Park Directors, 2018). While it is true that all of these participants were not necessarily motivated to enhance their well-being, they none the less received health benefits. It is also true that these data do not account for the millions of people who engaged in other health-promoting activities such as gardening, quiet reflection, wildlife observation, or socializing with friends or families in natural landscapes. It is easy to see that a substantial portion of today's citizens experience outdoor settings as a place of restoration, rejuvenation, and enhancement of well-being.

For many Indigenous and First Nations peoples, landscapes provide a critical connection to their lives, whether through actual subsistence living or a spiritual or traditional linkage to the past and present. According to the United Nations Permanent Forum on Indigenous Issues (UNPFII, n.d.), Indigenous refers to people who are native to a particular environment, with unique traditions, culture, language, and so on, distinct from dominant society, and who are descendants of groups who inhabited a region prior to colonization or other forms of conquest. Indigenous peoples make up 6% of the global population but 15% of the extreme poor, while simultaneously safeguarding over 80% of the world's biodiversity (The World Bank, 2020). Throughout the book, we have tried to include specific examples when referring to Indigenous people, but these examples do not mean that all Indigenous people are the same; nor do we intend to mythologize Indigenous people.

We also consider the experiences of other people of color and the histories of oppression and displacement that may contribute to differing experiences of the natural world than what is expressed in dominant narratives. We sometimes use the acronym BIPOC (Black, Indigenous, People of Color). This acronym emerged as a way of centering the unique experiences of Black and Indigenous peoples in relation to White supremacy, particularly in the USA, while also acknowledging similarities—especially in terms of marginalization—of the non-White experience (The BIPOC Project, n.d.).

Whatever the underlying needs, values, and reasons, the interaction between landscapes and human health involves a broad array of experiences, settings, and beliefs. Framing this interaction in terms of health and well-being is both timely and critical. As we experience a global pandemic, accelerating effects of climate change, and an intensification of the movement for racial justice in the USA and abroad, the role of the natural environment in our personal and collective well-being becomes increasingly clear.

Framing societal and research issues

This book approaches the linkage between natural landscapes and human health through the lens of two guiding questions, the first considering the various ways nature benefits human health from both historic and contemporary perspectives, and the second considering the mechanisms through which this relationship occurs. In doing so, we consider the ways societies and cultures have mediated our relationship with the natural world over time, and the ways human health and planetary health are intertwined.

Among other ways, this book examines these influences by providing an overview of what is currently known about specific variables, such as physical activity in natural landscapes, as well as discussing some of the past and current theories that seek to explain how these connections actually work. The book provides a bridge between what we do (individually and collectively) in natural settings and how those actions impact our health and our relationships with the natural world. Our hope is that the information presented here empowers students and professionals to learn more and to be part of the rich dialogue occurring in many disciplines to help find ways to increase well-being for all people. We want readers to think critically about research and be able to analyze and evaluate the results. The bottom line, based on the undertaking of this book and the experience of the authors, is that nature has been and continues to be essential and incredibly positive for human life, and that mutualistic and reciprocal connections with nature will positively influence human development, health, and well-being.

Structure and key features

This book serves a unique niche by recognizing the positive health-related aspects of interactions between landscapes and people. Moreover, it provides a broad overview of historical dimensions, theoretical underpinnings, research findings, implications for practice, and future perspectives. This information is presented in eight chapters. Chapter 1 provides an overview of the book, the underlying assumptions, and definitions of terms. Chapter 2 "Human Perceptions of Nature" examines the historical trajectory of human relationships with nature and the role of worldviews in influencing our perceptions and actions. Chapter 3 "Natural Landscapes and the Health Crisis" enlarges the discussion surrounding the relationship between issues such as changing climate and human health. Chapter 4 "Theories and Concepts: Linking Landscapes and Health" summarizes the theoretical foundations underlying the human health and natural landscape research.

Chapter 5 "Outcomes, Benefits, and Opportunities: Western Research Trends" surveys research trajectories and presents additional findings. Chapter 6 "Applications: Facilitating Healthy Connections with Nature" explores a variety of ways to facilitate connection with natural landscapes for specific populations and settings and highlights relevant cultural practices and frameworks. Related to this, Chapter 7 "Connecting with Landscapes: Intentional Access to Green Space" looks at approaches to conservation, preservation, and intentional design strategies for integrating nature into everyday life. Finally, Chapter 8 "Conclusions and Desired Future: Take a Park, not a Pill" provides a snapshot of future possibilities, anticipated societal needs, and the role that landscapes should play. The book ends with a list of guiding principles for a healthier and more sustainable future.

Where applicable, chapters highlight implications for practice to allow readers to draw connections between the chapter material and its manifestation in contemporary life. To broaden the scope of these applications and to provide global perspectives, chapters also feature a sidebar from a guest author describing human–natural landscape connections in their own country or region.

Who is This Book For?

The relationship between natural landscapes and health involves all beings and certainly all humans. The many forms of human and landscape interactions have received a substantial amount of interest from academic and professional disciplines, ranging from adventure therapy to urban planning. Beyond the purview of scholars, however, groups such as recreation professionals, conservation organizations, healthcare professionals, parents, and educators consider themselves stakeholders in understanding how landscapes influence health. Simply put, this book is designed for a wide range of students, academics, researchers, planners, and practitioners from a variety of disciplines and backgrounds.

We hope that this book helps readers to:

- be more predisposed to integrating nature into their personal and professional lives;
- invoke a deeper understanding of the research regarding the health benefits of landscapes, including methods and critiques, to stay current and able to assess future research;
- consider ways to implement action, whether through activities such as structured programming or legislation; and
- renew their appreciation for the natural world.

References

Andrews, M. and Gatersleben, B. (2010) Variations in perceptions of danger, fear and preference in a simulated natural environment. *Journal of Environmental Psychology* 30(4), 473–481.

Blonna, R. (2012) *Coping with Stress in a Changing World*, 5th edn. McGraw-Hill, Boston, Massachusetts.

Bruni, C.M., Chance, R.C., Schultz, P.W. and Nolan, J.M. (2012) Natural connections: bees sting, snakes bite, but they still are nature. *Environment and Behavior* 44(2), 197–215.

Bullard, R. and Wright, B. (2012) *The Wrong Complexion for Protection: How the Government Response to Disaster Endangers African American Communities*. NYU Press, New York.

Charles, C. and Louv, R. (2020) Wild hope: the transformative power of children engaging with nature. In: Cutter-Mackenzie-Knowles, A., Malone, K. and Barratt Hacking, E. (eds) *Research Handbook on Childhoodnature: Assemblages of Childhood and Nature Research*. Springer, New York, pp. 395–415.

Cronon, W. (1996) The trouble with wilderness: or, getting back to the wrong nature. *Environmental History* 1(1), 7–28.

Ewert, A., Mitten, D. and Overholt, J. (2014) *Natural Environments and Human Health*. CAB International, Wallingford, UK.

Foley, R. and Kistemann, T. (2015) Blue space geographies: enabling health in place. *Health & Place* 35, 157–165.

Franco, L., Shanahan, D. and Fuller, R. (2017) A review of the benefits of nature experiences: more than meets the eye. *International Journal of Environmental Research and Public Health* 14(8): 864.

Gallagher, W. (1993) *The Power of Place: How Our Surroundings Shape Our Thoughts, Emotions, and Actions*. Poseidon Press, New York.

Harper, N.J. and Dobud, W.W. (2021) *Outdoor Therapies: an Introduction to Practices, Possibilities, and Critical Perspectives*. Routledge, New York.

Hartig, T., Mitchell, R., De Vries, S. and Frumkin, H. (2014) Nature and health. *Annual Review of Public Health* 35, 207–228.

Johnson, D., Ambrose, S., Bassett, T., Cummery, D., Isaacson, J., *et al.* (1997) Meanings of environmental terms. *Journal of Environmental Quarterly* 26, 581–589.

Kim, G., Song, J. and Jeong, G. (2011) Neuro-anatomical evaluation of human suitability for rural and urban environment by using fMRI. *Korean Journal of Medical Physiology* 22, 18–27.

Kimmerer, R.W. (2015) Nature needs a new pronoun: to stop the age of extinction, let's start by ditching "it". *Yes!* 30 March. Available at: https://www.yesmagazine.org/issue/together-earth/2015/03/30/alternative-grammar-a-new-language-of-kinship/ (accessed 23 December 2020).

King, Y. (2017) Healing the wounds: feminism, ecology, and the nature/culture dualism. In: Scott, B.K., Cayleff, S.E., Donadey, A. and Lara, I. (eds) *Women in Culture: an Intersectional Anthology for Gender and Women's Studies*. Wiley Blackwell, Oxford, pp. 309–314.

Kuo, M., Browning, M., Sachdeva, S., Lee, K. and Westphal, L. (2018) Might school performance grow on trees? Examining the link between "greenness" and academic achievement in urban, high-poverty schools. *Frontiers in Psychology* 9.

Lariviere, M., Couture, R., Ritchie, S., Cote, D., Oddson, B., *et al.* (2012) Behavioural assessment of wilderness therapy participants: exploring the consistency of observational data. *Journal of Experiential Education* 35(1), 290–302.

Maller, C., Townsend, M., Pryor, A., Brown, P. and St. Leger, L. (2006) Healthy nature healthy people: 'contact with nature' as an upstream health promotion intervention for populations. *Health Promotion International* 21(1), 45–54.

Mantler, A. and Logan, A. (2015) Natural environments and mental health. *Advances in Integrative Medicine* 2, 5–12.

McDougall, C.W., Quilliam, R.S., Hanley, N. and Oliver, D.M. (2020) Freshwater blue space and population health: an emerging research agenda. *Science of the Total Environment* 737: 140196.

Mitten, D. (2004) Adventure therapy as a complementary and alternative therapy. In: Bandoroff, S. and Newes, S. (eds) *Coming of Age: the Evolving Field of Adventure Therapy*. Association of Experiential Education, Boulder, Colorado, pp. 240–257.

National Association of State Park Directors (2018) Statistics for 2018 Annual Information Exchange. Available at: https://www.stateparks.org/about-us/ (accessed 23 December 2020).

National Geographic (n.d.) Landscape. Available at: https://www.nationalgeographic.org/encyclopedia/landscape/ (accessed 23 December 2020).

Outdoor Foundation (2018) *Outdoor Recreation Participation Report, 2018*. Outdoor Foundation, Boulder, Colorado.

Pergams, O. and Zaradic, P. (2008) Evidence for a fundamental and pervasive shift away from nature-based recreation. *Proceedings of the National Academy of Sciences of the United States of America* 105(7), 2295–2300.

Razani, N., Hills, N., Thompson, D. and Rutherford, G. (2020) The association of knowledge, attitudes and access with park use before and after a park-prescription intervention for low-income families in the U.S. *International Journal of Environmental Research and Public Health* 17(3): 701.

Sorvig, K. (2002) Nature/culture/words/landscapes. *Landscape Journal* 21(2), 1–14.

Sport England (2015) Getting Active Outdoors: a Study of Demography, Motivation, Participation and Provision in Outdoor Sport and Recreation in England. Available at: https://sportengland-production-files.s3.eu-west-2.amazonaws.com/s3fs-public/outdoors-participation-report-v2-lr-spreads.pdf (accessed 16 May 2021).

Statistics Canada (n.d.) Participation in outdoor activities. Available at: https://doi.org/10.25318/3810012101-eng (accessed 28 December 2020).

Swanwick, C., Dunnett, N. and Woolley, H. (2003) Nature, role and value of green space in towns and cities: an overview. *Built Environment* 29(2), 94–106.

Taylor, D. (2014) *Toxic Communities: Environmental Racism, Industrial Pollution, and Residential Mobility*. NYU Press, New York.

The BIPOC Project (n.d.) About Us. Available at: http://thebipocproject.org (accessed 23 December 2020).

The World Bank (2020) Indigenous Peoples. Available at: https://www.worldbank.org/en/topic/indigenouspeoples (accessed 23 December 2020).

United Nations Permanent Forum on Indigenous Issues (UNPFII) (n.d.) Indigenous People, Indigenous Voices. Factsheet. Available at: https://www.un.org/esa/socdev/unpfii/documents/5session_factsheet1.pdf (accessed 28 December 2020).

United States Department of Health and Human Services (n.d.) Healthy People 2030: Neighborhood and Built Environment. Available at: https://health.gov/healthypeople/objectives-and-data/browse-objectives/neighborhood-and-built-environment#:~:text=Goal%3A%20Create%20neighborhoods%20and%20environments,their%20health%20and%20well%2Dbeing.&text=Healthy%20People%202030%20focuses%20on,work%2 (accessed 28 December 2020).

Williams, F. (2017) *The Nature Fix: Why Nature Makes Us Happier, Healthier, and More Creative*. WW Norton & Company, New York.

World Health Organization (WHO) (n.d.) Social Determinants of Health. Available at: https://www.who.int/health-topics/social-determinants-of-health#tab=tab_1 (accessed 28 December 2020).

World Health Organization (WHO) (2020) Preamble to the Constitution of the World Health Organization, forty-ninth edition. *Official Records of the World Health Organization*. WHO, Geneva, Switzerland. License: CC BY-NC-SA 3.0 IGO.

2 Human Perceptions of Nature

Actually, it doesn't make evolutionary sense for trees to behave like resource-grabbing individualists. They live longest and reproduce most often in a healthy stable forest. That's why they've evolved to help their neighbors.
~Suzanne Simard, PhD, forest ecologist who furthered theories about mother trees and intra- and interspecies nutrient sharing

While many readers likely enjoy time in nature and want to protect natural environments, in general, Western cultures historically have had violent and extractive relationships with natural landscapes. This chapter explores the worldviews held by early humans through to today, responding to questions such as "Was humans' relationship with nature always violent?" and "Did early humans feel in 'survival mode' against nature?" While it would be impossible to fully represent the diversity of worldviews at any given point in time, let alone throughout the history of humanity, it is useful to capture broad shifts in worldviews as they occurred over millennia.

What Are Worldviews?

Worldviews are the assumptions and beliefs that help people make sense of the complex world around them. On a practical level, having a worldview increases our understanding of our place and relationship to everyone and everything within our sphere and can therefore offer us security and comfort. One's worldview is personal. Though because it is conceptualized by social, cultural, and environmental interactions, we tend to share a **paradigm**, or a collection of stories, with the people or groups of people we live with, creating a collective or dominant worldview used to explain life, the world, and how we should be in the world. These shared views, or societal worldviews, shape behavior, politics, relationships, institutions, and the totality of our opinions and therefore how people act in and as a group.

As different worldviews become dominant, they influence our thoughts or perspectives about issues, which influences the overall direction of development of that area. In fact, history is interpreted through worldviews, and history itself is usually an essentialist and rejection process (see Mitten, 2021). As history (which is a subset of events and people) is told and recorded, it becomes part of the culture and is maintained by it, whether accurate or not. For example, large-scale archeological evidence of warfare dates back to less than 7000 years ago, but a dominant view today, supported by history selected for history books, is that defense and warfare are inevitable and part of human life (and death). Therefore, the USA, in particular, dedicates large budgets towards military readiness.

Worldviews and science

Worldviews are ontological in that they refer to a way of being and knowing about the world. In this way, they influence science and can differ from science. Worldviews (people's beliefs)

DOI: 10.1079/9781789245400.0002

direct what scientists study, the questions they ask, what data are gathered, and how they are valued (Harding, 2015). As humans, we need to question and challenge our and others' worldviews as we learn more. Do our actions stem from beliefs influenced by understanding the value of combining compassion with rigorous science or from other conditioning?

An example of the way scientific questions influence and are influenced by worldviews can be found in the study of race. In the early 1900s, scientists with a White-supremacist worldview attempted to demonstrate intellectual differences between races to support the assertion that some races were superior to others. This was also attempted between genders (Bleier, 1984) and was about proving supremacy. Race is not a scientific classification but rather a term coined to rationalize exploiting other humans (Painter, 2013). Scientists now agree that there are no biologically different human races, though sociopolitical structures and the public have been and continue to be deeply influenced by this construct, perpetuated by early pseudoscientific studies.

Similarly, climate change has become political, and some people's beliefs are driven by worldviews that discount science, while other people's worldviews are driven by compassion and science. Science confirms that human-caused climate change is real and that we need to reduce carbon emissions and curb consumption. To complicate this issue further, another common current worldview tells us that science contains the answer to humans' problems through technology—in other words, many people think that we can continue current levels of consumption and simply find technological solutions to our material resource needs, such as building stronger levies to deal with increasingly more destructive storms. A different worldview might see technology as a way to aid us in consuming fewer resources while living more mutualistically with natural environments. Examples of this would include enhancing public transportation options, creating greener immediate environments, and using video conferencing in lieu of long-distance travel. These choices are connected to the ways we relate to our natural landscapes. If the dominant worldview tells us that nature primarily functions as a source of materials for us to use, then we are more likely to lean into a consumptive culture. If the dominant worldview (or our personal one) tells us that we are a member of a larger ecological community, then perhaps we'll spend more time and energy interacting with and protecting that community in our local spaces and places. Some societies have retained an ecological community worldview despite the increasingly materialistic and destructive worldviews of dominant powers. It is possible to learn from these ecologically-minded people as we consider our desired future.

Worldviews and natural landscapes

Humans hold paradigms or worldviews for how we perceive our relationship with natural landscapes. Our social and physical environments—our landscapes—influence these perceptions. Currently, we are in the largest mass land migration of any known species, as humans have and continue to migrate to cities and urban areas. How might people's urban dwelling affect their beliefs, feelings, and actions around natural landscapes?

As humans spend more time in built environments, our worldviews change, including our values about life-giving landscapes. While for numerous people ecology has become a household word, in day-to-day life many people forget that we are part of ecological systems and intertwined with nature. Our actions now negatively affect the clean air and water as well as the healthy soils we need to live.

While worldviews contribute to humans' security and comfort, they do not necessarily portray an accurate relationship between humans and landscapes. For example, a Western cultural bias is to see early and current humans as being in survival mode against nature. Early people were active, encountered environmental challenges, and had different technology than we have today, but there is no reason to believe that they thought of themselves in a survival mode. In fact, artifacts point to early cultures being peaceful and egalitarian, with enough free time to create copious art.

What Is Civilization?

Anthropologist Margaret Mead interpreted a broken and healed human femur as a first sign of civilization. Her response surprised many anthropologists who were certain she would cite tools and buildings. Finding that healed femur meant people demonstrated compassion and community-mindedness—it takes up to 6 weeks for a femur to heal, and people have to stay put and help each other for that to happen. Mead emphasized that compassion and tending to others indicate civil and caring people. Following Mead, one could argue, as Jane Goodall and others have, that chimpanzees, whales, elephants, and many other animals who extend compassion in their kin units and beyond are civilized.

On the other hand, Thomas (1984) made a case for civilization being "virtually synonymous with the conquest of nature" (p. 25). Evidence of this embedded view of nature as needing to be tamed and controlled is manifested profoundly in the founding of the USA on individual rights and freedom for rich White men, where power and control over the land also extended to control of women and enslaved people. Reflecting on this current and historical reality, Nils Olaf Vikander's (2007) observation seems particularly poignant: "It is a paradox that the waves of European immigrants escaping constrictive societies did not shape nations with freedoms extended into nature" (p. 18). He might have added enslaved and Indigenous people and women to "nature."

In 2020, the world, exemplified by the elections in the USA, was in an existential crisis about values and the direction of the human race. Worldview clashes included issues of racial and gender justice, food security, gun control, women's reproductive rights, and COVID-19 pandemic behavior (e.g. whether or not to wear a mask). There were clear differences between countries governed by women and those not. Some see material gains, technology, and urban life as hallmarks of civilization, but too often these "advances" have come at the expense of other peoples and the natural world and create unhealthy conditions such as poor air, water, and soil quality. We authors encourage you to keep Margaret Mead's interpretation of civilization in mind when examining the history of worldviews, as well as when intentionally shaping your own future worldview.

A History of Humans' Worldviews

While throughout history there have always been multiple worldviews circulating at the same time, for the purpose of this book, we identify five major historical stages of worldviews or cosmological stories describing dominant society's perceptions of humans' relationship to nature. These are: (i) nature embodiment; (ii) sacred cycles; (iii) nature–culture duality; (iv) mechanical universe; and (v) modern technology. The year 2020 represents a crossroads.

We periodically learn more about historical worldviews as new data are discovered. For example, over time, enough evidence has accumulated to say that *Homo erectus* intentionally used fire over a million years ago. In 2020, from a Neolithic burial site in Jordan, archeologists unearthed 10,000-year-old flint figurines interpreted to mean their culture revered nature. These artifacts help confirm a worldview during that time of respect for life's interrelationships with nature. To aid with context, other geologic and archeological time periods are included in Table 2.1. Different fields of study name time periods according to their particular frame of reference, and the start/end times vary. Therefore, readers are encouraged to learn the relationships people had to their landscapes during these stages and to place less emphasis on exact dates.

Nature embodiment stage (enchanted cosmos: valuing birth, death, reciprocity)

Early *Homo sapiens* mutualistically developed with flora and fauna as part of ecosystems. Heavily influenced by their constant entanglement in their natural landscapes, these first humans observed and experienced nature as a system and allowed nature's cycles (stars, seasons, migratory paths) to generate a rhythm for their lives. Walking about 20 km daily, human bodies and brains grew to work well with movement. Humans primarily gathered their food, supplementing 3–4% with found meat or hunting. The grandmother hypothesis developed by Hawkes (2004) and other researchers asserted that it was not "man the hunter" but grandmothers with abundant ecological knowledge who were responsible in humanity's early days for keeping the extended family and tribe fed. These long-lived women's progeny was selected for, resulting in more longer-lived women to keep their families fed as time went forward.

Archeological evidence in pollen cores show that for over 120,000 years, people have lived and practiced agriculture on what is now Australia, including purposeful burning in the Lake George catchment (Builth, 2014). Oral histories from Indigenous Elder Uncle Max Harrison and other story keepers confirm this long agricultural history, and that their ancestors arrived from Antarctica when the two continents were connected—differing from many anthropologists who believe that all humans started in Africa.

By the nature embodiment stage, humans' regulation was controlled by the vagus nerve, numerous hormones, microbes, and other chemical reactions. Through effecting neuronal cells, the hormone oxytocin promotes trust, social bonding, empathy, forgiveness, and altruism. Oxytocin, a powerful modulator of brain functions, is both a hormone and a neurotransmitter that makes people more responsive to social cues and social feedback and improves the accuracy of reading people's emotions (Meyer-Lindenberg *et al.*, 2011). This hormone-driven attachment helped children stay close to kin as they learned to navigate their landscapes and helped family groups stay intact to help each other. Conditioning and oxytocin play roles in the strong maternal–child bonds in mammals, as well as the lasting psychological connectedness between humans and natural landscapes. Recent studies show people given supplementary oxytocin are more inclined to view themselves as interconnected with other people and living things (Van Cappellen *et al.*, 2016). Cooperating and trusting each other and their landscapes is a capacity that has allowed the human species to thrive. Bowlby (1988), Maslow (1971), and others say that humans need to attach and belong to survive (Fitzgerald, 2020). Attachment is a survival mechanism driven by hormones and the microbes within humans' bodies and reinforced through healthy human relationships.

Table 2.1. There have been five major paradigms in the known history of humanity, each with its dominant worldview as gleaned from artifacts, middens, and oral and written history and literature. Today, humans are at a crossroads.

Stage and cosmological story	Beginning date	Other geologic and archeological period interfaces	Dominant worldviews in relation to nature
Nature embodiment Enchanted cosmos: valuing birth, death, reciprocity	~300,000 years ago	Pleistocene Epoch; Prehistoric; Old Stone Age; Middle Stone Age; Early and Middle Paleolithic; Behavioral Modernity	Embodied sense of landscapes; sense of oneness with nature's cycles (stars, seasons, migratory patterns), which generated a rhythm of life. Health was being in rhythm with natural cycles, closely tied to their landscapes.
Sacred cycles Earth-centered: revered nature, awe, compassion, cooperation, values of belonging	~50,000 years ago	Pleistocene Epoch; Reindeer Age; New Stone Age; Mesolithic; Neolithic (began 12,000 years BCE)	Most cultures were egalitarian, exhibiting care and cooperation and respect for natural systems, femaleness, and birth. People thrived in their landscapes, revealing time affluence. Disease was being out of rhythm with natural cycles.
Nature–culture duality Domination of nature: warfare and slavery	~6,000 years ago	Holocene Epoch; Bronze Age; Iron Age; Neolithic; Ancient Egypt; Roman Period; Dark Ages	Worldviews bifurcated: many continued to revere and live in nature's cycles, while others created a nature–culture duality, including a belief that nature (and other humans) should be cultivated and subdued. Western people's health moved to the purview of religious leaders and men.
Mechanical universe Domination of nature: extractive, exploitive economies based on scarcity	~14th century	Holocene Epoch; Renaissance; Enlightenment; Age of Reason; Classical Modernity; Late Modernity; The First Industrial Revolution ~1760–1870; The Second Industrial Revolution 1870–1914	Both Judeo–Christian values and science supported a belief in separateness from nature. Science worked to mechanistically control natural processes. Nature, children, and conquered people are seen as commodities for growth. Colonization by Europeans and others ensued. Economies externalized environmental costs.

Modern technology Estrangement from nature: disordered attachment and mental health issues	~1900 CE	Holocene Epoch; Flight Age; Space Age; Computer Age; Information Age; Digital Age; The Third Industrial Revolution (1980s)	Quantum physics and systems thinking poke holes in mechanical thinking; externalized environmental costs caused huge health consequences, especially for poor and people of color; many Indigenous people and others lobby for the rights of nature.
Crossroads Liminal state: the mechanical universe competes with quantum physics and an organic and regenerative universe	~2020 CE	Anthropocene[a] Epoch; The Fourth Industrial Revolution (2020s)	Climate change and racial and environmental justice continue as worldwide issues. The COVID-19 pandemic kills millions worldwide. In 2020, 75% of the world's populations use herbs for basic healthcare needs (World Health Organization, 2020).

[a]As of September 2020 (Mathews, 2020), the Anthropocene is still a proposed, not accepted, name for a geologic epoch marked by human impacts on global ecosystems. Some scientists call the current period the Anthropocene, while others say that as humans, we are too close to name a new epoch. Still others assert that naming a new epoch after humans continues the exceptionalism that precipitated the crisis of this current era. Other proposals include staying with Holocene longer or Ecozoic (house of life) to capture a shared cosmological journey with all beings and replace despair at the destruction of nature with hope and a story where humans recover their creative orientation to the world.

Humans' sense of presence and embodiment of their landscapes helped them live with the rhythms and cycles of the earth, as well as with a certain amount of unpredictability. People's daily activities were entangled with nature, and this engagement with nature promoted well-being. Additionally, shamanic practices evolved in Africa, Australia, and with the Reindeer people in the Far North that integrated health with reciprocity with their landscapes. Healing emphasized coming back into harmony with natural cycles and rhythms, later, in some cultures symbolized by the medicine wheel.

Sacred cycles stage (revered nature)

In the sacred cycles stage, humans continued to be entwined with their landscapes. They gathered or grew about 96% of their food, though the balance shifted in favor of growing. Many cultures tended certain plants to increase species diversity, selectively harvested specific parts of a plant so it grew back prolifically, and replanted seeds (Turner et al., 2000). They related to their landscapes using systems thinking, which continues to be reflected in Indigenous knowledge from many traditions.

While herbal medicines were used more than 60,000 years ago with the Reindeer people in Northern Europe, in Iraq, and other places, during this time many more societies developed holistic healing practices intertwined with their landscapes. Ayurveda, Native American, and Tibetan medicine are among the many nature-based systems of medicines developed and continue to be used today. Healing was seen as reconnecting with the natural rhythms of the landscape that helped regulate the natural rhythms within us. Reflected in the remains of many ancient societies is their learning through observation and experientially about natural systems.

These thriving cultures, marked by time affluence, evidenced an upsurge of visual arts, as well as care for the elderly and infirm, systematic burials, and game playing. The earliest discovered flutes were made during this stage. Sculptures of birth-giving goddesses and pottery figures of bird-headed deities and sacred serpents all honored the regenerative powers of nature. The proliferation of music and art suggests these people were doing more than just surviving.

Carol Lee Flinders' (2003) research demonstrated the reciprocal relationship early people had with the natural world, with one another, and with their deities. This complemented their society's core values of intimate relationship with the land, empathetic relationship with animals, self-restraint, generosity, egalitarianism, playfulness, and non-violent conflict resolution. Current research supports that these traits develop or strengthen in people when they spend time in natural landscapes.

Archeologist Marija Gimbutas' detailed research about the images and symbols she unearthed from just before the Bronze Age illuminated those people's attention to birth and compassion and provided evidence for a creative, stable, and peaceful human civilization well into what some call the Neolithic or agricultural period. She deduced from thousands of artifacts that the female body was a metaphor for nature; the womb was sacred, renewing itself with the cycle of birth. Living in the cyclical rhythm of stars and seasons, egalitarian cultures were the norm in this thriving nature-revering society (Gimbutas and Marler, 1991). Seasonal rites, initiation rituals, and other forms of participation in the sacred ceremonies of life that followed nature's rhythms were mirrored in cave art (Noble, 1993).

Gimbutas outlined the worldview Old European societies had of the universe and the divine and their embodied understanding of the Gaia hypothesis: "The multiple categories, functions, and symbols used by prehistoric peoples to express the Great Mystery are all aspects of the unbroken unity of one deity, a Goddess who is ultimately Nature herself" (Gimbutas and Marler, 1991, p. 223).

India: Inner and outer lives are influenced by landscapes
By Nandini Kumar and Tanya Ginwala

From pristine white-sand beaches to dense tropical deciduous forests, vast arid deserts to the icy Himalayan glaciers, India's diversity and uniqueness extends to its physical landscapes. Despite being a land of striking contrasts and contradictions, the common thread running through centuries are the physical features that have breathed life into our culture and social structures.

Like most civilizations around the world, our ancestors shared a sacred relationship with the land and lived in harmony with nature. Be it the tribal hunter community in Nagaland that seeks guidance from the cliffs (which they consider the protector of animals) or the devout Hindu who finds solace in the evening *arti* (prayers) by a river, our inner and outer lives have been heavily influenced by the landforms that surround us.

Our landscapes symbolize what we hold dear and externalize the deeply felt emotions of our relationship with the divine—we see *peepal* trees (under which the Buddha attained enlightenment) as keepers of spirits, mountains as our ancestors, and rivers as the female energy that eventually feeds every one of us. The river Ganga, for example, is not only a lifeline for millions in India but is also seen as a "mother," a sacred goddess with healing powers, and is a recurring theme in Bollywood movies.

We have a complex, multifaceted relationship with our landscape. Our physical, spiritual, and social lives often interchange swiftly, making it challenging to separate one from the other. For centuries, the Indigenous Adivasi communities in India have sustained and nurtured an interdependent relationship with nature. This way of being has become the impetus for grassroots conservation movements around the world. The Bishnoi community of Rajasthan, for instance, is known for protecting several plants and animals such as the *khejri* tree and the *chinkara* (Indian gazelle), even at the cost of their own lives.

Continued

Sacred groves and *sthalavriksha* (temple trees) are a common sight in most village communities. Sacred groves (known by several names, depending on the region they are found) are patches of forest devoted to the local deity that the Indigenous communities have protected and revered as sacrosanct for many generations. They usually support endemic species of flora and fauna and play a crucial role in maintaining the ecological and agroecosystem balance of the region.

In India, time is seen as cyclical, aligned with the cycles of the sun, the moon, the stars, and the rest of nature. The traditional Indian medicine system Ayurveda is known for being a holistic system of herbal medicines that inculcates religion and philosophy. Ayurveda finds its roots in nature and considers the whole universe to be made up of five essential building blocks that constitute all life forms—the *Panchamahabhutas*. These are: (i) *akasha* (ether); (ii) *vāyu* (air); (iii) *teja* (fire); (iv) *aap* (water); and (v) *prithvi* (earth).

As kids, we would often hear stories about people who retired from their *sansarik* (worldly) lives and retreated to the mountains in search of a higher truth. Today, like much of the rest of the world, our relationship with nature is more tenuous than ever before. Many people seem to have forgotten our essential and dependent connection to nature and have lost our way by adopting ways of life that are fragmented and disconnected from the land. May our rich history of nature connection and reverence serve as a map to help us, and the rest of the world, find our way back to nature, and ourselves.

Nature–culture duality stage (power over nature, including other humans)

The nature–culture duality stage began many societies' dislocation and alienation from nature. This stage seemed to be a transitional time from egalitarian cultures who embodied their landscapes to patriarchal societies who saw themselves as separate and above or dominant over nature.

Archeologists started seeing signs of warfare about 6000 years ago, as well as the first artifacts of a father god. Written histories about this time period depict the dominant society as hierarchical with kings, merchants, farmers, and enslaved people. During this stage, the social structure changed and people differentiated into specific occupations. Patriarchy, fueled by the church, created a hierarchy of men over women and rational knowledge over relationships. A worldview evolved believing it was okay to amass power and control and use food surpluses to dominate other humans. Race was invented as a way for people labeled White to enslave people labeled Black.

However, while wars and attempts to conquer other peoples were common in certain areas, colonialists represented a small part of the world population. Most people continued to live in cooperation and mutuality with their landscapes *with reverence for nature*, though most histories leave this out.

During this time period, nature-based systems of medicines continued to be the primary healing modalities. A huge culture clash with worldviews was displayed in the last four centuries of the Middle Ages (peaking in the late 15th century into the 17th century) when over 6 million healers, called **wise women** (women skilled in healthcare through working with herbs and remedies directly from nature), were killed in Europe as that culture transitioned to the Age of Reason.

As the climate became more temperate, people domesticated animals, shed their nomadic lifestyle, built permanent homes, and accumulated material goods. There was a growth in population, and people lived in closer contact to one another than in earlier stages. The majority of the world's population appeared to shift to agrarian lifestyles—though cultures had been harvesting wild grains and cultivating plants and animals for millennia. Some societies continue today to be nomadic, primarily gathering their food.

The split between the church and science, the move toward a belief in mechanization, and the quest for more resources for growth and power amplified the antagonistic relationship many humans were developing with nature and with one another.

Mechanical universe stage (resource extraction)

The mechanical universe cosmological story exemplifies a world that runs like clockwork according to a set of physical laws. The mechanical worldview championed rational objectivity instead of sympathetic intuitive understanding of nature and spirit, leading to ever-increasing pressure on natural resources and reliance on the environment to absorb the polluting effects of industrialization.

In Western countries, by the time of the Renaissance, people divided into two primary factions: one aligned with the Judeo–Christian church and one aligned with the new positivist and then post-positivist science. Both factions viewed nature as a commodity for human use—to be used, cultivated, and subdued. When transitioning to an industrialized society, nature was seen as the source of raw materials for growth—an endless means to an endless end. Slavery, child labor, and indentured servitude jump-started the time period.

Through warfare and imperialism, Europeans invaded and colonized many lands, supplanting Indigenous people who lived there (often cooperatively). Indigenous people in the USA were separated from their landscapes, including their food and medicine sources (e.g. in the 1700s, Mohawk corn crops were routinely burned to starve them).

The idealization of materialism and wealth accumulation launched a preoccupation with symbols of wealth rather than actual measures of health. Land was accumulated, and material wealth was used as power rather than shared as had been the case for millennia. These values led to the destruction of natural landscapes, an economy dependent on consumer spending and growth, and an assembly line educational system.

The dominant worldview about nature in the mechanical stage can be summarized as reductionism, resource extraction, and binary and dichotomous thinking, resulting in a culture of consumption driven by materialism and consumerism. The industrial ages, catalyzed by the invention of the fossil-fuel-powered steam engine propelled people into a time of rapid change.

Fueled by the Cartesian mechanistic model and Newtonian physics, and exacerbated by new technologies, people believed they could learn functions and then control nature's processes. The belief prevailed that matter is inert—and that humans can rearrange it. This idea of separateness was used to argue for individual liberties (for White people) and to criticize cooperative cultures. Fewer pockets of Indigenous people continued their reciprocal relationship with nature; many were simply overrun by the industrial machine.

With the advent of printing, the adage "history is written by the winners" became operational. What is written down and by whom creates enduring, essentialist, accounts of history. Very little during the mechanical universe and modern technology stages was written about Indigenous people or people who continued to live close to and embodied in the landscapes. What was written was usually by non-Indigenous people and often was inaccurate. Throughout history, many people have continued to live with the land, eschewing the ideals of consumerism, capitalism, and conflict.

Modern technology stage (estrangement from nature)

The modern technology stage (1900–2020) was filled with technological discoveries, including flight, living in space, and wearing computers on wrists, with a continued dependence on fossil fuels and an extractive economy based on growth. Technology was revered and viewed as the rescuer for environmental problems caused by the Industrial Revolution, as well as the answer to comfort-related needs and health troubles, even as new and more physical and mental health issues arose.

The Western cultural worldview promoted individual pursuit and acquisition of material wealth as the pathway to happiness and freedom. Over time, the paradigm of individualism, competition, and dominance became like a runaway train and directly caused the current worldwide ecological predicament. Especially after World War II, growth, integral in Western policy and capitalism (which is often conflated with democracy), was aggressively exported to the world at large.

A worldview of superiority of humanity over natural landscapes spurred massive overconsumption, beyond what the natural landscapes could sustain. People became the dominant force of change to the earth's systems. Meanwhile, poverty and food shortages created crises for billions of people in the world whose lives were oppressed by other people's material consumption, adding another set of complex social, economic, and ecological impacts. Profound health inequalities were linked to these uneven distributions of resources and opportunities (World Health Organization, 2020).

People in modern societies became further distanced from outdoor landscapes, and a pervasive Western narrative of the time was that people were separate from one another and the rest of the natural world. As people moved from farms to cities, from producing their own food to buying it, from spending time in natural landscapes to being surrounded by buildings, many people felt as though this was true. However, humans are never actually separate from nature; humans are superorganisms and with our microbiomes rely on the air, water, and nutrients for survival. Instead of being separate from nature, people were unaware of their land-based roots and of being part of the earth's ecosystem. Roszak (1995) said a deep despair underlies Western culture. Humans may have lost that "value of belonging" that research today confirms people need and feel when in nature.

Secure attachment to caregivers and nature is essential for healthy human development. Walant (1999) explained that in Western culture, attachment needs of children have been sacrificed for the cultural norms of separation and individuation, setting the stage for normative abuse of children and nature. Children with attachment disorder generally lack impulse control, may be violent, and tend toward addictions, which exemplifies much of Western society. It is not a lack of connection; it is the lack of a healthy connection (D'Amore and Mitten, 2015).

Through a dysfunctional relationship, including avoidant attachment (Bowlby, 1988) and fear, many humans treated nature with criticism and contempt, which primed people to stay hypervigilant, conflictual, guarded, and non-receptive to healthy relationships with nature. These behaviors led to anxiety, exhaustion, and immune diseases—many of the stress-related diseases of this period (Mitten, 2017).

Beginning in the early part of the 20th century, influenced by the dominance frame of mind, settlers from European countries and the USA used natural landscapes for training and recreation, which included "conquering" mountains previously held in spiritual esteem by local people (and renaming them, e.g. Denali to Mount McKinley; Chomolungma—"Goddess of the Wind"—and Sagarmatha—sky's head—to Mount Everest). A postmodern view of men having become weak and needing toughening led to outdoor programs using natural landscapes as a testing ground, reinforcing an adversarial relationship with nature. Risk taking, domination, and egocentric attitudes were explicitly or implicitly encouraged. People returned home thinking more about what they could achieve rather than relationships.

The wilderness movement in the USA combined romanticism, environmental protection, and imperialism. White male preservationists believing the dominant worldview of nature being separate from humans acted to preserve and protect natural landscapes by keeping them separate from human civilization. The Wilderness Act of 1964 illustrated that humans wanted to be in a relationship with landscapes, while also considering themselves separate, by defining:

> A wilderness, in contrast with those areas where man [sic] and his own works dominate
> the landscape, is hereby recognized as an area where the earth and its community of life are
> untrammeled by man [sic], where man [sic] himself is a visitor who does not remain.
> (Anon, 1964, Section 2(c))

Preservationists from settler descent, such as Marsh, Thoreau, and Muir, largely overlooked that Indigenous people lived in these lands and had healthy relationships with natural landscapes. As they campaigned for preservation via a national park designation, Muir and Roosevelt described Yosemite Valley as a pure, wild paradise, eliding the fact that creating the national park required evicting the Miwok, a tribe who had tended and lived with the land in Yosemite for thousands of years. The Miwok were just one of many native tribes that were removed from what would become a protected area, national park, or "wilderness" to be enjoyed by primarily White people. This degree of disregard for the human experience is inherent in colonial thinking.

While some groups romanticized the environment, others vilified it. For example, The Weather Channel in the USA relentlessly told about the horrors that "nature" imposed upon humans, adding to feelings of animosity toward nature. Driven by media-inspired fear, people witnessed and experienced nature as violent, causing many people, especially in developed countries, to become nature-phobic.

By the mid-1900s, scientists and writers like Ellen Swallow Richards, Florence Nightingale, Aldo Leopold, and Rachel Carson, all of whom understood ecosystems, expressed the importance of the interface of nature and human health, encouraging people in politics and at home to clean up environmental pollution as well as take time to experience the beauty and awe of nature. Rachel Carson's (1962) *Silent Spring*, warning about big agriculture and the use of pesticides, helped usher in the 1970s' environmental movement. Globally, practitioners of outdoor and environmental education, believing in the value of being outdoors, educated people about their natural landscapes and environmental ethics. Numerous folks learned outdoor living and traveling skills and drew links between these practices and the health of people and the environment.

While technologies enabled humans to live longer lives, they have radically changed human interactions with surrounding landscapes. Digital devices combined with urbanization, agricultural intensification, and other aspects of modern life inhibit people from forming personal connections with landscapes. Without a felt connection to natural landscapes, people are less likely to care about nature and have been shown to be less compassionate in general, resulting in a negative feedback loop where care diminishes and destructive practices toward nature and other humans increase.

Toward the end of the 20th century, more Indigenous people who kept the knowledge of the mutual dependency between nature and humans at the forefront of their culture, including reciprocal nourishment, were able to speak out against violations to themselves and their ancestral homelands. Several countries, including Ecuador and New Zealand, gave human rights to nature (Dunbar-Ortiz, 2019).

Crossroads (liminal state)

Following years of reckless pursuit of technological fixes and unchecked capitalism, 2020 provided many signs that humanity may be at a crossroads of sustaining human life. The global pandemic, the global call to address racial injustices, and intensifying environmental concerns (e.g. climate change including carbon dioxide (CO_2) production, loss of biodiversity and deforestation, ocean acidification, plastic pollution, and lack of clean and accessible water) have put the world and its people in a liminal state with an uncertain future.

People's physical and mental distance from natural landscapes, exacerbated by technology, is removing humans ever further from the immediate consequences of their actions on natural systems. This has led to dramatic human-caused changes to natural systems, more natural disasters (e.g. hurricanes and wildfires), and a build-up of negative health consequences because of humans' self-polluted living environment (e.g. CO_2, methane, and chemical toxins).

Increasing mental health issues worldwide, including the rise of gun violence, death by suicide rates, self-harm, and addictions, exposed the mental health crisis, now widely understood by professionals as a social crisis (Woods et al., 2019). Humans' unhealthy and unacknowledged relationship with nature fuels this predicament.

Worldviews and Choice and/or Where Do We Go From Here?

There may always be mystery around the beginnings of life, including human life. Indigenous people and Western folks have their cosmology stories (an aspect of their worldview) to understand the "great mystery" of our human journey, including who we are, how we got here, and where we are headed. The stories people hear or are privileged by a society influence the ways they interact with all elements of landscape, including other humans. Many Indigenous groups use cosmology stories to teach worldviews that help people feel a sense of belonging and understand their responsibilities in sustaining life. Western science is devoid of a cosmology story that creates civic or responsible action for people (e.g. the Big Bang theory only describes material origins). The impact of the last 6000 years has been to reinforce estrangement of people from their landscapes, as well as to reinforce a value of manufactured and non-nature-based goods. Western people continue to believe that technology can save them from environmental devastation.

Humans' disregard of or superior feelings over nature may be a result of fear. As humans lost the value of belonging (Flinders, 2003), they experienced inner doubts and distress; they did not feel loveable and capable, the two ingredients necessary to sustain healthy relationships (Clarke, 1998). A number of Western people, concerned that humans have lost emotional and affective connection with the processes of life embedded in the emergence of the cosmos, have articulated universe stories that combine the evolutionary sciences and cultural traditions to offer Western people a path forward to generate a flourishing future (Lorde, 2004; Berry and Berry, 2009; Elgin, 2010; Swimme and Tucker, 2011; Macy, 2021). These authors encourage people to consciously construct a worldview that values life and replaces people's, sometimes subconscious, despair at the destruction of nature with hope (discussed in Chapter 6, this volume). Given our cognitive abilities as humans, we can consciously create a worldview that provides sustainability for the human species and a deep connection to all life. Each one of us descends from people who had intimate and reciprocal relationships with the flora, fauna, rocks, and soil, and healthily reconnecting with the natural world, especially within the realm of dominant culture, may be part of a solution that moves us toward planetary health and well-being. The remainder of this book focuses on this approach.

References

Anon (1964) Wilderness Act of 1964. 16 U.S.C. 1131–1136, 78 Stat. 890. United States of America.

Berry, T. and Berry, T.M. (2009) *The Sacred Universe: Earth, Spirituality, and Religion in the Twenty-First Century*. Columbia University Press, New York.

Bleier, R. (1984) *Science and Gender: a Critique of Biology and its Theories on Women*. Pergamon Press, Oxford.

Bowlby, J. (1988) *A Secure Base: Parent–Child Attachment and Healthy Human Development*. Basic Books, New York.

Builth, H. (2014) *Ancient Aboriginal Aquaculture Rediscovered: the Archaeology of an Australian Cultural Landscape*. Lambert Academic Publishing, Saarbrücken, Germany.

Carson, R. (1962) *Silent Spring*. Houghton-Mifflin, Boston, Massachusetts.

Clarke, J.I. (1998) *Self-Esteem: a Family Affair*. Hazelden Foundation, Center City, Minnesota.

D'Amore, C. and Mitten, D. (2015) Nurtured nature: the connection between care for children and care for the environment. In: Thomas, P.L., Carr, P., Gorlewski, J. and Porfilio, B. (eds) *Pedagogies of Kindness and Respect: On the Lives and Education of Children*. Peter Lang. New York, pp. 113–128.

Dunbar-Ortiz, R. (2019) The International Indigenous People's Movement: a site of antiracist struggle against capitalism. In: Satgar, V. (ed.) *Racism After Apartheid: Challenges for Marxism and Anti-racism. Democratic Marxism Series*. Wits University Press, Johannesburg, South Africa, pp. 30–48.

Elgin, D. (2010) *The Living Universe: Where Are We? Who Are We? Where Are We Going?* Berrett-Koehler Publishers, San Francisco, California. Available at: https://duaneelgin.com/wp-content/uploads/2010/11/The_Living_Universe_EXCERPT.pdf (accessed 23 December 2020).

Fitzgerald, J. (2020) Attachment to irreplaceable others. In: Rhodes, P. (ed.) *Beyond the Psychology Industry*. Springer, Cham, Switzerland, pp. 23–33.

Flinders, C. (2003) *Rebalancing the World: Why Women Belong and Men Compete and How to Restore the Ancient Equilibrium*. HarperCollins, San Francisco, California.

Gimbutas, M. and Marler, J. (1991) *The Civilization of the Goddess: the World of Old Europe*. Harper, San Francisco, California.

Harding, S. (2015) *Objectivity and Diversity: Another Logic of Scientific Research*. University of Chicago Press, Chicago, Illinois.

Hawkes, K. (2004) Human longevity: the grandmother effect. *Nature* 428(6979), 128–129.

Lorde, A. (2004) *Conversations with Audre Lorde*. University Press of Mississippi, Jackson, Mississippi.

Macy, J. (2021) *World as Lover, World as Self: a Guide to Living Fully in Turbulent Times*. Parallax Press, Berkeley, California.

Margulis, L. (1998) *Symbiotic Planet: a New Look at Evolution*. Basic Books, New York.

Maslow, A.H. (1971) *The Farther Reaches of Human Nature*. Viking Press, New York.

Mathews, A.S. (2020) Anthropology and the Anthropocene: criticisms, experiments, and collaborations. *Annual Review of Anthropology* 49, 67–82.

Meyer-Lindenberg, A., Domes, G., Kirsch, P. and Heinrichs, M. (2011) Oxytocin and vasopressin in the human brain: social neuropeptides for translational medicine. *Nature Reviews Neuroscience* 12(9), 524–538.

Mitten, D. (2017) Connections, compassion, and co-healing: the ecology of relationship. In: Malone, K., Truong, S. and Gray, T. (eds) *Reimagining Sustainability in Precarious Times*. Springer, New York, pp. 173–186.

Mitten, D. (2021) Critical perspectives on outdoor therapy practices. In: Harper, N.J. and Dobud, W.W. (eds) *Outdoor Therapies: an Introduction to Practices, Possibilities, and Critical Perspectives*. Routledge, New York, pp. 175–187.

Noble, V. (ed.) (1993) *Uncoiling the Snake: Ancient Patterns in Contemporary Women's Lives*. HarperCollins, San Francisco, California.

Painter, N.I. (2013) *Southern History Across the Color Line*. University of North Carolina Press, Chapel Hill, North Carolina.

Roszak, T. (1995) Where psyche meets Gaia. In: Roszak, T., Gomes, M. and Kanner, A. (eds) *Ecopsychology: Healing the Earth, Restoring the Mind*. Sierra Club Books, San Francisco, California, pp. 1–20.

Swimme, B.T. and Tucker, M.E. (2011) *Journey of the Universe*. Yale University Press, New Haven, Connecticut. Available at: www.journeyoftheuniverse.org (accessed 23 December 2020).

Thomas, K. (1984) *Man and the Natural World: Changing Attitudes in England 1500–1800*. Penguin Books, Harmondsworth, New York.

Turner, N.J., Ignace, M.B. and Ignace, R. (2000) Traditional ecological knowledge and wisdom of aboriginal peoples in British Columbia. *Ecological Applications* 10(5), 1275–1287.

Van Cappellen, P., Way, B.M., Isgett, S.F. and Fredrickson, B.L. (2016) Effects of oxytocin administration on spirituality and emotional responses to meditation. *Social Cognitive and Affective Neuroscience* 11(10), 1579–1587.

Vikander, N.O. (2007) Feet on two continents: spanning the Atlantic with friluftsliv? In: Henderson, B. and Vikander, N. (eds) *Nature First: Outdoor Life the Friluftsliv Way*. Natural Heritage Books, Toronto, Canada, pp. 8–22.

Walant, K. (1999) *Creating the Capacity for Attachment: Treating Addictions and the Alienated Self*. Jason Aronson, Northvale, New Jersey.

Woods, M., Mavklin, R., Dawkins, S. and Martin, A. (2019) Mental illness, social suffering and structural antagonism in the labour process. *Work, Employment and Society* 33(6), 948–965. https://doi.org/10.1177/0950017019866650

World Health Organization (WHO) (2020) Preamble to the Constitution of the World Health Organization, forty-ninth edition. *Official Records of the World Health Organization*. WHO, Geneva, Switzerland. Licence: CC BY-NC-SA 3.0 IGO.

3 Natural Landscapes and the Health Crisis

... it is not enough to weep for our lost landscapes; we have to put our hands in the earth to make ourselves whole again. Even a wounded world is feeding us. Even a wounded world holds us, giving us moments of wonder and joy. I choose joy over despair.

~Robin Wall Kimmerer, PhD, botanist, professor, and member of the Citizen Potawatomi Nation

Nature can be amazing! Watching a sun rise or sun set encourages feelings of awe, joy, and contentment for many people. Experiencing mountain vistas or staring at the Milky Way can inspire a sense of being part of something larger than oneself. Of course, these descriptions are generalizations based on research with specific populations, and any one person's experience is inherently subjective and their cultural and personal background critical to their understanding the full context of their feelings.

Many astronauts and cosmonauts have described a cognitive shift in awareness when they see earth from space. Frank White (2014) described an overview effect:

It refers to the experience of seeing firsthand the reality that the Earth is in space, a tiny, fragile ball of life, "hanging in the void," shielded and nourished by a paper-thin atmosphere. The experience often transforms astronauts' perspective on the planet and humanity's place in the universe. Some common aspects of it are a feeling of awe for the planet, a profound understanding of the interconnection of all life, and a renewed sense of responsibility for taking care of the environment. (White, 2014, p. 2)

Research in the concept of awe reports that people feel a sense of transformation and connectedness as they view scenes in nature. As wonderful as feelings of awe are, as in all relationships, there are ups and downs. Nature does not always seem nice, nor should that be the case. As people who travel in the outdoors understand, bears, ravens, and other animals can eat your food, and avalanches, excessive heat, and biting insects are elements that travelers work with to be safe. Yet a rainbow at the end of torrential downpour can offer beauty and hope.

Indigenous people, philosophers, and an increasing number of scientists agree that humans don't merely live on the earth; rather, we are part of the earth interconnected with everything else, even the cosmos, though many humans have grown to believe they are separate from nature. The violent and extractive relationship Western societies have had with natural landscapes over the past 7000 years or so (described in Chapter 2, this volume) has exacerbated this narrative of being separate from nature. As people migrated to cities, the lack of regular contact with and comfort in nature led many people to express pervasive fear and mistrust of the natural world. These events have ruptured many humans' relationships with nature. Believing one is separate from nature yet knowing one depends on nature has led to many humans having a complicated and multidimensional relationship with their landscapes.

Humanity faces a host of existential challenges, from the COVID-19 pandemic to plastics. Climate change, causing a Siberian town north of the Arctic Circle to reach 100°F (38°C), gun violence, escalating social and economic inequity, and segregation

DOI: 10.1079/9781789245400.0003

are all understood as matters of public health and related to the degradation of landscapes. Humans and landscapes are environmentally overburdened with toxic chemicals. A bulletin on 8 September 2020 reported eight out of ten deaths in Europe are because of pollution (European Environment Agency, 2020). Research suggests that urban living is associated with higher rates of psychiatric disorders, with frequencies as much as 50% higher for conditions such as mood disorders (Peen *et al.*, 2010). Because of population growth and urban migration, 7.8 billion humans are living more interconnected lives than ever before, as well as with more violence, addictions, and poverty.

Owing largely to growing concern and public outcry over deteriorating environments where rivers caught fire and cities were thick with smog in the 1960s, Western scientists developed the interdisciplinary field of bioclimatology to study the effects of the physical environment on living organisms, including humans. This led to an understanding that the earth had reached a carrying capacity for many pollutants; this meant nature could not recover and humans could not survive with the trajectory of the earth's pollution. After a too-brief reprieve that included beneficial environmental policy and legislation that has saved millions of lives, politicians and other decision makers used misleading information to focus instead on economic growth for the wealthy. Humans are again at a crossroads, though now the pollution and problems are more insidious and widespread.

There is no doubt that humans have polluted and changed the natural environment to such an extent that we are in crisis or an age of consequences. What humans choose to do or not do next depends on their worldviews. Many Indigenous people and scientists assert that to survive, humans must recognize and nurture their symbiotic relationship with the earth. At odds with the worldview that nature is a commodity, Indigenous scientist Kimmerer (2013) says a lack of reciprocity sits at the heart of the ecological crises, aggravated by endless consumption of goods and ceaseless taking from nature without giving anything in return. Kimmerer advocates for a shift in perspective to one of healthy relationships rather than overconsumption.

This chapter focuses on how landscapes can be harmful to human health and well-being and suggests possible strategies for reparation and to regain a reciprocal relationship with landscapes. Climate change, Indigenous practices, and ecological grief are discussed.

Aotearoa: Māori and *pākehā* value ancestral lands and biophilic cities
By Susan Houge Mackenzie

Aotearoa/New Zealand (land of the long white cloud) is home to diverse landscapes, including volcanoes, fiords, glaciers, beaches, forests, lakes, plains, and mountain ranges. New Zealanders (Kiwis) place high value on their natural resources, and one-third of Aotearoa is protected for conservation. Due to millions of years of isolation, unique flora and fauna, such as giant snails and flightless birds, coexist in an area roughly the size of Colorado, USA. New Zealand (NZ) has a rich history of valuing natural landscapes for adventure and well-being, driven in part by its challenging landscapes and geographical isolation. Ancestors of Indigenous Māori discovered Aotearoa on exploratory voyages from Polynesia, navigating solely by ocean currents, stars, and winds. Since the early 1900s, NZ schools have embraced outdoor physical activity and adventure recreation to build character as part of mainstream education. Iconic Kiwi explorers, such as Sir Edmund Hillary, have fueled NZ's cultural valuing of adventure and reputation as the birthplace of innovative adventure activities, such as bungy jumping. Many Kiwis view natural landscapes as their "playgrounds" and place high value on access to nature for personal development and for

Continued

sustaining social and family connections via shared outdoor experiences. These values are reflected by legislative and investment priorities, such as the Department of Conservation maintaining nationwide public trail and hut networks. The capital, Wellington, is a global leader in the biophilic cities movement, a global network of cities pursuing a vision of "natureful cities." Biophilic cities like Wellington seek to protect the myriad well-being benefits of urban biodiversity and wild urban spaces. Wellington is also home to Zealandia's Centre for People and Nature, which researches nature and human well-being.

Typical *pākehā* (New Zealanders of European descent) values associated with natural landscapes center on character building, personal development, and social connections. In contrast, Māori have a more holistic value system in relation to the natural environment and human well-being. Like many Indigenous cultures, Māori clearly articulate links between healthy ecosystems and people's cultural, physical, and spiritual well-being. Māori recognize that ecosystems require diversity to function and maintain sustainability. The importance of ancestral lands, water, sites, *wāhi tapu* (sacred place), and other *taonga* (treasure) is a matter of national importance in Aotearoa under the Resource Management Act. As such, Māori values associated with natural landscapes and features must be recognized by law.

Traditional Māori values reflect complex and holistic understandings of how natural landscapes support human well-being. The *tangata whenua* (people of the land) view themselves as one with the natural world. The people, the land, the sea, and all living creatures are members of the same family with direct *whakapapa* (genealogical) connection through ancestors. Nature is central to, rather than separate from, Māori identity and well-being. Linkages between the natural world and Māori are explained through *whakapapa* and mythology, which represent how Māori are descended from and are connected to the natural world. Therefore, reciprocity and caring for nature is central to human well-being and survival as every person, place, and object has *mauri* (life force). For example, a body of water may have *mauri*, or positive energy, that enables marine life to thrive. If its *mauri* is damaged, the lake will not provide food for a community. Thus *mauri ora* reflects the need to protect natural areas from harm. The Māori value *kaitiakitanga* also identifies fundamental connections between human well-being and the natural world. Māori view humans as guardians of the natural environment to ensure the survival of future generations. These links between human well-being and natural landscapes are epitomized by NZ legislation granting geographic features, such as Mount Taranaki, legal rights. This status means if someone harms one of these natural areas, it is legally the same as harming the local *iwi* (tribe). From this perspective, human and environmental well-being are often considered one and the same in Aotearoa.

Landscapes Are Not Always Healthy for Humans

Wild plants and animals can be harmful to individuals and societies. Movies, such as *Into the Wild* (Penn *et al.*, 2007), hype the dangers of poisonous plants, playing into fear of nature perceived by many Westerners. Globally, however, plants are an uncommon cause of significant poisoning. Deaths from plant poisoning are rare in the industrialized world, accounting for fewer than 50 deaths/year, and while there are more deaths in the developing world, almost all of them are death by suicide or homicide (Eddleston and Persson, 2003). Tobacco use, on the other hand, causes more than 5 million deaths/year, and acute poisoning with pesticides is a global public health problem accounting for as many as 300,000 deaths worldwide every year (Goel and Aggarwal, 2007).

Poisoning by animal venom, including snakes, spiders, scorpions, and marine creatures, is common, but rarely is there significant morbidity and mortality. Sharks kill fewer than a dozen people annually worldwide, bears fewer than 50 people, and large cats close to 1000 people, as do crocodiles. Snake venom, however, kills tens of thousands of people, especially in India and parts of Africa (Schiermeier, 2015). Mosquito-transmitted diseases (though not the mosquito's bite) kills about 500,000 people annually. Even though a small number of the 3500 mosquito species in the world carry these deadly diseases, with human-caused climate change, places usually too cold, like Canada, may be affected by mosquito-transmitted diseases in the future. In 2018, nine vector-borne human diseases were discovered or introduced for the first time in the USA and territories (Ng *et al.*, 2019).

Microbes, such as severe acute respiratory syndrome coronavirus 2 (SARS-CoV-2), cause of COVID-19, have influenced human history. The European 1348 plague was estimated to have killed a third to a half of the population. These sorts of microbes were the infectious diseases Europeans brought to the Americas, Australia, and southern Africa that killed local populations and irreversibly altered local flora and fauna. Widespread use of antimicrobial agents and chemicals has selected for more resistant populations of microbes and more resistant insect vectors, which ultimately harms human populations, especially vulnerable ones. As nature's ecosystems become disrupted and disturbed, the opportunity for microbes to jump from other animals to humans increases and is predicted to happen more frequently.

By and large, with knowledge about how to interact with the plants and animals, hazards in natural landscapes can be minimal. Because many Western people view the outdoors as wild, scary, or dangerous, media tends to reinforce this eco- or biophobia paradigm (Estok, 2018). For example, "Summer dangers: Outdoor activities raise risk of illness, injuries" headlined an article that opened:

> Picnics, campouts, hiking, fishing, gardening, and many more activities are all popular in the summer months. And lurking behind every one of those activities and many more are dangers that can quickly have you humming the summertime blues, and sometimes there ain't no cure.
> (Belt, 2006, para. 3)

Once into the article, the writer talks about a woman who walked off a pathway in the dark near her house after gardening and stepped on a snake that bit her. She was in the hospital for 2 days and on crutches for 2 weeks from the offending copperhead snake. The article continued that about two snakebites/year are seen in that emergency room with no reported deaths.

It is excellent public policy to help educate people on how to avoid snakebites. However, it encourages the public to be afraid of outdoor environments by using sentences such as the one that came next: "Snakes aren't the only danger lurking behind seemingly innocuous activities" (Belt, 2006, para. 12). The writer then talks about injuries from mowing, using hedge clippers, and chainsaws. It might be the same as recommending to avoid hunting because you might shoot yourself or your friend. The danger comes from the human's tools, not nature. A final example from the article was getting sick from salmonella by eating a precut melon, a danger created by the food supply chain. None of these examples, except the snakebite, relate to innate dangers of natural landscapes and instead come from human inventions for convenience.

Our attitudes about natural landscapes impact health. Encouraging fear and mistrust of natural landscapes can be harmful for people because it encourages a state of hyperarousal, causing hypervigilance (exaggerated intensity of behaviors in order to detect threats) when thinking about or interacting with natural landscapes. This state and subsequent behavior can lead to anxiety, exhaustion, and a diminished immune system.

Harm from dangerous plants and animals and non-mechanical accidents in natural settings is small compared with the toxic contaminants humans have put in these landscapes. Natural disasters such fires, storms, floods, and tornados are legitimate concerns, which become heightened as population densities increase and human-caused climate changes intensify these disasters. From 2009 to 2019, natural disasters killed an annual average of 60,000 people globally (0.1% of total deaths), though a single disaster in a particular year has killed up to 3 million people (Ritchie and Roser, 2019). Humans' polluting of natural landscapes harm and kill millions of people each year. Sometimes policies made to help overall well-being unintentionally cause more illness and death.

Health Risks from Polluted Environments

The United Nations Human Development Index identifies the most important requirement for eradicating poverty (transitioning to a middle-class life) as access to energy, which means about 3000 kWh per person/year (Conca, 2017). China decided in 1992 to build about 600 coal-fired power plants, along with other energy sources, lifting 500 million Chinese into the middle class. However, toxic emissions from their coal-fired plants, an unintended consequence, kills over 300,000 people/year and harms millions, leading to a huge unforeseen burden on their healthcare system (Conca, 2017).

The US Clean Air Act of 1970 (1970 CAA) reduces US air pollution by 70% and is the single piece of legislation that has saved the most US lives in history (EPA 2020);[1] still, about 60,000 primarily poor, Black, and Latinx people die per year because of air pollution in the USA (State of Global Air, 2020). Without equivalent legislation, developing countries average about ten times more people dying per kilowatt of energy produced than in the developed world. Still, the USA pays $200 billion to make and deliver coal electricity, and then pays over $350 billion in healthcare costs related to coal production and use (Conca, 2017). Polluted air and contaminated water and land kill more people worldwide each year than smoking, hunger, natural disasters, war, murder, acquired immunodeficiency syndrome (AIDS), tuberculosis, and malaria combined. The World Health Organization estimated that non-communicable diseases (NCDs) comprise nearly two-thirds of the 12.6 million deaths caused by the environment each year, translating globally that 23% of all deaths might be prevented through healthier environments (Landrigan et al., 2018). These adverse health effects disproportionately impact disadvantaged populations and are often in urban environments.

Exposure science—the process of estimating or measuring the effects of contact with chemical, physical, or biological agents—helps further understanding of how time in particular landscapes may cause, prevent, or improve adverse health outcomes. Measuring the effects of potentially harmful agents in the environment is as necessary as measuring benefits of exposure to landscapes. For example, particulate matter air pollution, the leading environmental risk factor for the global burden of disease, can be measured on an area-wide and individual level with wearable devices such as MicroPEM or microenvironmental air samplers. Some of these tools, small enough to fit on wristbands, are used in real time to monitor physiological responses to find out at what point the harm done by pollution might outweigh well-being benefits gained from exercise in the outdoors (Dons et al., 2017). In some areas in the USA, children are advised not to play in their yards because of soil pollution (Anderson, 2020; Sullivan and Green, 2020). Research about the effects of exposure to toxins in the environment reinforces the need to attend to pollution and climate change causes, as well as to know where spending time outdoors might be harmful or helpful to well-being.

Climate Change

Scientists agree that climate change has and will cause severe disruptions as well as exacerbate current problems such as poverty, violence, and human migration. Even though millions of people will migrate in response to climate change, no one will be able to escape its effects. Droughts affect about 25% of the world's population (Ritchie and Roser, 2019) and are an impetus to migration. The Intergovernmental Science-Policy Platform on Biodiversity and Ecosystem Services (IPBES) concluded that the same human activities that drive climate change and biodiversity loss also drive pandemic risk. The COVID-19 pandemic, in part, is a result of climate change coupled with exotic and illegal animal trade. Climate change first and most strongly impacts poor, Indigenous, and people of color (Taylor, 2014).

Operating under the auspices of the United Nations, since 1988 the Intergovernmental Panel on Climate Change (IPCC) (2019) provides policy makers with scientific assessments of climate change and its implications and potential future threats to guide adaptation and mitigation options. They report global warming and the ensuing rapid climate change is caused by a combination of factors, most notably fossil fuel usage, deforestation, and farming livestock, which add methane and carbon to the atmosphere, thereby blocking the escape of heat from the earth's surface. These changes happen at all times and scales—large and small—and in all geographies. Climate change is either implicated in or a direct cause of many of the environmental issues we currently face, including wildfire expansion, ocean level rise, glacier melt, and the loss of biodiversity.

Fire

Fires, both a product of climate change and a contributor to climate change, impact natural ecosystems and sectors of the economy such as agriculture, tourism, transportation, and insurance. Warming climates have caused wildfires to intensify in severity and effect. Places not typically thought of as fire sensitive, such as the Mediterranean, have become hotspots. Boreal forests in Sweden have seen megafires. Wildfires in Siberia have increased in frequency and severity over recent decades. The area burned by fires in the USA has significantly increased in the last 15 years, and in Alaska, temperatures are increasing twice as fast as the rest of the country, further fueling fires there (Dos Passos Coggin, 2019).

These bigger, hotter fires, through negative feedback loops, cause more climate change. This escalation, occurring more rapidly in the Arctic than elsewhere, causes the release of large amounts of planet-warming greenhouse gases (*The Economist*, 2020). The resultant dark scars and soot increases the amount of heat the region absorbs from the sun, causing more drought, which increases its susceptibility to fire and intensifies the next season. High temperatures, drought, and increased tree mortality due to bark beetle infestation, which has underlying climate drivers, all contribute to the worldwide increase in fires. Changing precipitation patterns has increased the growth of low vegetation, prone to combustion when dry and serving as kindling for larger fires. In recent years, an increase in the temperature of the Indian and Southern Oceans causing dry and warmer weather in Australia (which per capita has the largest share of greenhouse gas emissions of any country in the world) sparked debilitating fires in the summer of 2019/2020 (*The Economist*, 2020).

The Amazon has experienced three widespread droughts in the 21st century, igniting massive wildfires. Both drought and fires expose local communities to hazardous air quality that damages human health, including causing diseases of the respiratory system (Machado-Silva *et al.*, 2020). Globally, the Amazon forests greatly affect the weather system and control the regional climate that maintains the Amazon ecosystem as well as the region's agroforestry and farming. It also functions as a carbon sink, though fires and deforestation have curbed that ecosystem service.

Ocean levels

At an increasing rate, the global sea level is rising due to thermal expansion as the oceans warm and there is increased melting of land-based ice, including glaciers and ice sheets. Changes in ocean current movement and speed cause site-specific sea level changes such as in Florida, USA, where the slowing of the Gulf Stream (another effect of climate change) causes sea level rise. Additionally, some areas contend with local sea level rise owing to the land sinking due to water consumption for drinking and agriculture (leaving empty space), wetlands sinking as they become drier and lose density, and downward pressure from building infrastructure in heavily populated areas.

Glaciers

Used as tourist attractions for centuries, some of the most dramatic and visual representations of climate change are melting and calving glaciers. Numbering somewhere between 200,000 and 400,000 worldwide, glaciers are often seen as something to measure and monitor to predict their movement and, in recent years, to predict ocean rise (melting land ice causes two-thirds of global sea rise) (Cazenave and Llovel, 2010).

Glaciers also have helped shape communities and people's place-based identities. Glaciologist Mary Jackson (2019) explored the heartfelt connections between people, place, and ice and how glacial changes impact communities. She explained that some people perceive glaciers as sentient—alive and breathing creatures—and talked about the level of care some people give to their glaciers, concluding that how we interact with our environment predicts how we care for our environment. For example, as glaciers melt, introspective questions arise such as "Can one still be Icelandic without land ice?" People's relationships with glaciers are tied to their identity.

While glaciers are melting at a faster rate than at any other time in human history, Jackson (2019) is not ready to say that we are losing the world's ice. Many variables influence the retreat and advance of glaciers—resulting in uncertainty in predicting the future of glaciers across the globe.

Biodiversity

Worldwide, countries are losing their ecosystems as natural landscapes are being replaced by human-built features and infrastructures (Bruni *et al*., 2017). Other areas, such as the Amazon, are being burned and cleared for cattle and crop production. Simply, complex ecosystems such as rainforests cannot be replanted.

Called the sixth mass extinction by scientists, billions of regional and local plant and animal populations have been lost, with many species losing up to 80% of their habitat. This biological annihilation is primarily caused by habitat destruction due to consumption patterns by industrialized nations and human population expansion. It is estimated that species are becoming extinct 100 times faster than they would without human impacts. Populations of wild animals have more than halved since 1970, while the human population has doubled (Wackernagel *et al*., 2000). Additional habitat destruction happens through invasion by species foreign to an area, toxic pollution, and overhunting. For example, a highly virulent wildlife disease, chytridiomycosis, whose recent spread has been facilitated by humans, has caused mass amphibian die-offs worldwide (Burrowes *et al*., 2019).

Like all plants and animals, amphibians' roles are critical to human and the earth's survival as we know it. Amphibians eat pest insects, benefiting agriculture and helping to minimize the spread of diseases such as malaria, Zika virus, West Nile virus, dengue fever, Lyme disease, and encephalitis. Without amphibians, these diseases would further strain various healthcare systems. In one example, India learned the economic benefit of frogs eating insects through experience. In the 1980s, India began exporting frog legs for food. The population of frogs dropped significantly and insect activity rose dramatically. The government made it illegal to export frog legs in 1987 because the cost of pesticides needed to control insect pests exceeded what they were receiving for the exported frogs.

Having porous and permeable skin and living in both land and water, amphibians are sensitive to pollutants and function as indicator species for environments becoming toxic for humans. Feeding amphibian tadpoles regulate the amount of algae, preventing bodies of water from developing algae blooms that would make them too toxic to drink or harvest food from. The list continues. Amphibian skin contains peptides already used in painkillers, high blood pressure medication, to block human immunodeficiency virus (HIV) transmission, and to treat antibiotic-resistant bacterial strains—a major public health problem worldwide.

Whether it is about values toward glaciers or amphibians, attitude matters. Human cultures have cherished amphibians as agents of life and good luck—is this ancient and outdated? Probably not. Using amphibians as an example, when their value to humans is illustrated, we see that when we destroy biodiversity, we harm ourselves. According to scientists, the earth is an organism, and each species has its role in the earth's systems functioning well (see Chapter 2, this volume).

Destruction Can Be Profitable

From pipelines to unsustainable development, the problems that threaten to overwhelm us have occurred as side effects of a system whose rapid growth is both encouraged at all costs and blind to natural limits. Our current economic system is designed so that some people profit from continued environmental destruction, which makes conversations about climate change challenging. For example, last-chance tourism has boomed in the past decades, encouraging people to visit glaciers and places that soon will be gone (Lemelin and Whipp, 2019; Miller *et al.*, 2020). Other people may benefit from earlier and longer growing seasons.

Potential profits from environmental destruction influence violence. In 2020, 127 known environmentalists including park rangers, Indigenous leaders, and grassroots activists were killed globally (Cox, 2018). Western colonizers' frontier mentality, a world-view of "conquer or be conquered," created this unsustainable global situation. Violence, including lateral and internal violence, signals a larger systemic breakdown of relation-ships. The violent degradation of natural landscapes as well as violence in communities results in trauma, and this trauma has seeped into culture.

Humans now need worldviews that enable us to be here for the long haul. From both a spiritual and a scientific perspective, care and reciprocity is integral to the healthy func-tioning of ecosystems. An understanding that all beings matter can guide reciprocal and compassionate behavior.

Indigenous Perspectives

In 2019, the IPBES noticed that Indigenous land, though it faced the same global pres-sures, was degrading less quickly. In that same year, University of British Columbia researchers, looking at biodiversity in Canada, Australia, and Brazil, found more species of birds, animals, and amphibians on land managed by Indigenous people, even greater than in national parks. While Indigenous people are 4% of the world's population, they manage or have tenure over about a quarter of the global land surface, and their lands may house at least 75% of the global biodiversity (Dinerstein *et al.*, 2019).

This suggests that learning from their knowledge, and expanding their stewardship, is necessary for a healthier world. Dinerstein *et al.* (2019) called for better protection for Indigenous communities and declared that global sustainability goals are more achievable by upholding existing land tenure rights, addressing Indigenous land claims, and carrying out supportive ecological management programs with Indigenous peoples.

Relationships are fundamental to life on every scale, and while the Western world might be awakening to and beginning to realize the importance of ecological relation-ships, Indigenous communities have understood the inherent nature of reciprocity for millennia. Kimmerer said:

> Reciprocal restoration is the mutually reinforcing restoration of land and culture such that repair of ecosystem services contributes to cultural revitalization, and renewal of culture promotes restoration of ecological integrity. Based on the indigenous stewardship principle that "what we do to the land we do to ourselves" restoration of land and culture are inseparable. This approach arises from a creative symbiosis between traditional ecological knowledge and restoration science, which honors and uses the distinctive contributions of both intellectual traditions. Reciprocal restoration recognizes that it is not just the land that is broken, but our relationship to it. Reciprocal restoration encompasses repair of both ecosystem and cultural services while fostering renewed relationships of respect, responsibility, and reciprocity. All flourishing is mutual.
> (Kimmerer, 2011, p. 258)

At its core, reciprocal restoration is relationship repair work. Restoring "right" rela-tionships to the land requires shifting humanity's self-focus and hierarchical placement above nature to realizing ourselves as horizontal to and interwoven with the circle of life.

Grief and Reconciliation

As Toni Morrison's thoughtful imagery conveys, given opportunity, nature can recover:

> You know, they straightened out the Mississippi River in places to make room for houses and livable acreage. Occasionally the river floods the places. "Floods" is the word they use, but in fact it is not flooding; it is remembering. Remembering where it used to be. All water has a perfect memory and is forever trying to get back to where it was.
>
> (Morrison, 1995, pp. 98–99)

When grappling with ways natural landscapes have been degraded, a host of feelings can overwhelm people—sorrow, outrage, despair—and some people go numb. As maintained in this book, humans are emotionally attached to their landscapes. Numerous cultures and ancient healing systems understand how foundational place attachment is to mental health (see Chapter 2, this volume). Following settler disruption, many Indigenous people expressed their feelings of loss in relationship to their land and continue to do so with recent climate change losses. Working with Inuit communities, Cunsolo and Ellis (2018) found that when melting glaciers prevented travel to significant cultural sites and engagement in traditional culture activities such as hunting and fishing, Inuit people's sense of place was disrupted and accompanied by strong emotional reactions, including grief, anger, sadness, frustration, and despair.

Researchers who document and monitor the extraordinary change coral reefs and other ecological areas have experienced are forming support groups online. They want spaces to express their feelings of grief and distress in response to the environmental destruction they witness.

Joanna Macy helps people renew their fractured relationship with the planet through healing ecological grief. She contends that grief is a legitimate response to the vast ecological destruction, which includes traumatized, stressed, and poisoned people who may live and work in polluted, toxic areas. Macy (2021) has said the most radical thing any of us can do at this time is to be fully present to what is happening in the world. Having worked with people since the 1970s on processing emotions around ecological loss, she has determined that feeling the grief—allowing one's heart to break—helps transform despair into clarity of vision and then constructive, collaborative action. Her goal is to help people be free of the assumptions and attitudes that threaten life on earth. She wants people to know that whatever the limitations of their life, they are free to choose the version of reality or story about the world they value and want to implement in their life. We can align with business as usual and continue to pressure the environment, we can enter into despair, or we can move to create a life-sustaining society.

Ecopsychologists understand that psychological processes bond humans with nature. In that relationship, people can feel many different emotions. Most recently, **ecological grief**—sorrow at the devastation of nature—has been a focus. Through ecotherapy (also called nature therapy and more—see Chapter 6, this volume) people explore their connections to their landscapes, including this sense of profound loss. Outdoor experiences with skilled leaders and therapists can help people change narratives of competition to ones of reciprocal, collective relationship and belonging, which influences ecological identity and environmental behaviors (see Chapter 4, this volume).

Time in nature can improve mental health outcomes, including helping to heal ecological grief. However, dominant culture severely underinvests in maintaining natural landscapes and biodiversity. Buckley *et al.* (2019) recognized that natural areas have a health services value, estimated to be US$6 trillion/year. This component of ecosystem services has been profoundly overlooked in conservation policy. Degrading mental health is costly for treatment, caregivers, lost work productivity, and antisocial behavior (e.g. crime and domestic violence). Chapter 6, this volume, describes a number of outdoor therapies, and sectors such as outdoor education, recreation, and tourism that deliver programs to help people spend quality time in nature. Protected area management agencies should partner with programs of this sort (see Chapter 7, this volume).

Working with ecological grief can help people move toward the action we need to heal our relationships with the earth. Solutions to problems have to involve the global community of all beings. The complexity of the world's challenges calls for an intersectional approach with extensive interdisciplinary and cross-sectoral collaboration including cultural perspectives. People have to be healthy enough to construct narratives that include appreciation and respect for landscapes, allowing for relationship intimacy and repair as needed.

COVID-19 and other diseases are symptoms of an exhausted planet, though people have not given up. Youth-led climate strikes are happening in many countries, and these young people have strong social networks from which to support each other. Let down by earlier generations, they are proactive about their future. We can learn from the youth and from Indigenous people who have embedded traditional wisdom and practices that honor the reciprocity between people and their natural surroundings.

> Climate change is not an enemy to be vanquished; it is a phenomenon deeply tied to our daily lived existence. It is part of the conversation our mixed up, beautiful, contrary, and imaginative people must have about who we are as a people and where we want to go.
>
> (Dr. M. Jackson, cited in Young, 2019)

Note

[1] The Trump administration gutted enforcement of the Act so the future is not reliably known.

References

Anderson, K.R. (2020) "Do not play" outdoor advisories: examining the impact of soil lead contamination in urban communities. Doctoral dissertation, Indiana University Bloomington, Indiana.

Belt, M. (2006) Summer dangers: Outdoor activities raise risk of illness, injuries. *Lawrence Journal-World* 26 June. Available at: https://www2.ljworld.com/news/2006/jun/26/summer_dangers_outdoor_activities_raise_risk_illne/ (accessed 27 December 2020).

Bruni, C.M., Winter, P.L., Schultz, P.W., Omoto, A.M. and Tabanico, J.J. (2017) Getting to know nature: evaluating the 1001 effects of the Get to Know Program in children connectedness with nature. *Environmental Education 1002 Research* 23(1), 43–62.

Buckley, R., Brough, P., Hague, L., Chauvenet, A., Fleming, C., *et al.* (2019) Economic value of protected areas via visitor mental health. *Nature Communications* 10(1), 1–10.

Burrowes, P.A., Carvalho, T., Catenazzi, A. and De la Riva, I. (2019) Amphibian fungal panzootic causes catastrophic and ongoing loss of biodiversity. *Science* 363(6434), 1459–1463.

Cazenave, A. and Llovel, W. (2010) Contemporary sea level rise. *Annual Review of Marine Science* 2, 145–173.

Conca, J. (2017) Pollution kills more people than anything else. *Forbes* 7 November. Available at: https://www.forbes.com/sites/jamesconca/2017/11/07/pollution-kills-more-people-than-any-thing-else/?sh=7b8b85641a35 (accessed 23 February 2021).

Cox, R. (2018) New data reveals 197 land and environmental defenders murdered in 2017. Global Witness blog, 2 February. Available at: https://www.globalwitness.org/en/blog/new-data-reveals-197-land-and-environmental-defenders-murdered-2017/ (accessed 18 November 2019).

Cunsolo, A. and Ellis, N.R. (2018) Ecological grief as a mental health response to climate change-related loss. *Nature Climate Change* 8, 275–281. Available at: https://doi.org/10.1038/s41558-018-0092-2 (accessed 28 December 2020).

Dinerstein, E., Vynne, C., Sala, E., Joshi, A.R., Fernando, S., *et al.* (2019) A global deal for nature: guiding principles, milestones, and targets. *Science Advances* 5(4): eaaw2869.

Dons, E., Laeremans, M., Orjuela, J.P., Avila-Palencia, I., Carrasco-Turigas, G., *et al.* (2017) Wearable sensors for personal monitoring and estimation of inhaled traffic-related air pollution: evaluation of methods. *Environmental Science & Technology* 51(3), 1859–1867.

Dos Passos Coggin, J. (2019) New report highlights Alaska's last five years of dramatic climate change. *Climate.gov*, 15 October. Available at: https://www.climate.gov/news-features/understanding-climate/new-report-highlights-alaska%E2%80%99s-last-five-years-dramatic-climate (accessed 23 February 2021).

Eddleston, M. and Persson, H. (2003) Acute plant poisoning and antitoxin antibodies: antivenoms. *Journal of Toxicology: Clinical Toxicology* 41(3), 309–315.

EPA (2020) Air Quality – National Summary. EPA United States Environmental Protection Agency, United States Government. Available at: https://www.epa.gov/air-trends/air-quality-national-summary (accessed 23 February 2021).

Estok, S.C. (2018) *The Ecophobia Hypothesis*. Routledge, New York.

European Environment Agency (EEA) (2020) Healthy Environment, Healthy Lives: How the Environment Influences Health and Well-being in Europe. EEA Report No 21/2019. Available at: https://www.eea.europa.eu/publications/healthy-environment-healthy-lives (accessed 1 January 2021).

Goel, A. and Aggarwal, P. (2007) Pesticide poisoning. *National Medical Journal of India* 20(4), 182.

Intergovernmental Panel on Climate Change (IPCC) (2019) *Climate Change and Land*. IPCC, Geneva, Switzerland.

Jackson, M. (2019) *The Secret Lives of Glaciers*. Green Writers Press, Brattleboro, Vermont.

Kimmerer, R. (2011) Restoration and reciprocity: the contributions of traditional ecological knowledge. In: Egan, D., Hjerpe, E.E. and Abrams, J. (eds) *Human Dimensions of Ecological Restoration: Integrating Science, Nature, and Culture*. Island Press, Washington, DC, pp. 257–276.

Kimmerer, R.W. (2013) *Braiding Sweetgrass: Indigenous Wisdom, Scientific Knowledge and the Teachings of Plants*. Milkweed Editions, Minneapolis, Minnesota.

Landrigan, P.J., Fuller, R., Acosta, N.J., Adeyi, O., Arnold, R., *et al.* (2018) The Lancet Commission on pollution and health. *The Lancet* 391(10119), 462–512.

Lemelin, H. and Whipp, P. (2019) Last chance tourism: a decade in review. In: Dallen, T. (ed.) *Handbook of Globalisation and Tourism*. Edward Elgar Publishing, Cheltenham, UK, pp. 316–322.

Machado-Silva, F., Libonati, R., de Lima, T.F.M., Peixoto, R.B., de Almeida Franca, J.R., *et al.* (2020) Drought and fires influence the respiratory diseases hospitalizations in the Amazon. *Ecological Indicators* 109: 105817.

Macy, J. (2021) *World as Lover, World as Self: a Guide to Living Fully in Turbulent Times*. Parallax Press, Berkeley, California.

Miller, L.B., Hallo, J.C., Dvorak, R.G., Fefer, J.P., Peterson, B.A. and Brownlee, M.T. (2020) On the edge of the world: examining pro-environmental outcomes of last chance tourism in Kaktovik, Alaska. *Journal of Sustainable Tourism* 28(11), 1703–1720.

Morrison, T. (1995) The site of memory. In: Zinsser, W. (ed.) *Inventing the Truth: the Art and Craft of Memoir*, 2nd edn. Houghton Mifflin, New York, pp. 83–102. Available at: https://blogs.umass.edu/brusert/files/2013/03/Morrison_Site-of-Memory.pdf (accessed 4 January 2021).

Ng, V., Rees, E.E., Lindsay, L.R., Drebot, M.A., Brownstone, T., *et al.* (2019) Could exotic mosquito-borne diseases emerge in Canada with climate change? *Canada Communicable Disease Report* 45(4), 98–107.

Peen, J., Schoevers, R.A., Beekman, A.T. and Dekker, J. (2010) The current status of urban–rural differences in psychiatric disorders. *Acta Psychiatrica Scandinavica* 121(2), 84–93.

Penn, S., Linson, A., Pohlad, B. (Producers) and Penn, S. (Director) (2007) *Into the Wild [Motion picture]*. Paramount Vantage, Paramount Studios, Los Angeles, California.

Ritchie, H. and Roser, M. (2019) Natural Disasters. *Our World in Data* November. Available at: https://ourworldindata.org/natural-disasters (accessed 28 December 2020).

Schiermeier, Q. (2015) Africa braced for snakebite crisis. *Nature* 525(7569), 299.

State of Global Air (2020) Explore the Data: Health Impact – Burden on Your Health – Plots. Available at: https://www.stateofglobalair.org/data/#/health/plot (accessed 23 February 2021).

Sullivan, M. and Green, D. (2020) Toward eliminating children's lead exposure: a comparison of policies and their outcomes in three lead producing and using countries. *Environmental Research Letters* 15(10), 103008.

Taylor, D. (2014) *Toxic Communities: Environmental Racism, Industrial Pollution, and Residential Mobility*. NYU Press, New York.

The Economist (2020) This year's Arctic wildfires are the worst on record, again. *The Economist* 7 September. Available at https://www.economist.com/graphic-detail/2020/09/07/this-years-arctic-wildfires-are-the-worst-on-record-again (accessed 30 December 2020).

Wackernagel, M., Linares, A.C., Deumling, D., Schulz, N.B., Sanchez, M.A.V. and Falfan, I.S.L. (2000) *Living Planet Report 2000*. WWF (World Wide Fund for Nature) Worldwide Network, Gland, Switzerland.

White, F. (2014) *The Overview Effect: Space Exploration and Human Evolution*, 3rd edn. American Institute of Aeronautics and Astronautics, Reston, Virginia. https://doi.org/10.2514/4.103223

Young, A. (2019) Dr. M Jackson on the Teachings of Glacial Beings /111. *For The Wild audio podcast*, 13 March. Available at: https://forthewild.world/listen/dr-m-jackson-on-the-teachings-of-glacial-beings111 (accessed 23 February 2021).

4 Theories and Concepts: Linking Landscapes and Health

> Nature matters to people. Big trees and small trees, glistening water, chirping birds, budding bushes, colorful flowers—these are important ingredients in a good life.
>
> ~Rachel Kaplan, PhD, environmental psychologist and author of attention restoration theory

Philosophers, writers, poets, religious figures, scientists, and even politicians have sung the praises of nature at varying points over the past millennia. More recently, researchers have theorized about the importance of human connection to landscapes. This chapter explores some of the theories and concepts related to the ways people believe landscapes benefit human well-being. Existing theories derive from a variety of academic fields, ranging from biology to geography to psychology, and represent a range of perspectives.

Theories and concepts are used to construct knowledge and derive from worldviews, while also constructing or reinforcing worldviews. A **theory** is a set of statements or principles that seek to explain a group of facts or phenomena (Bickman and Rog, 2009). A theory must be testable, and it should provide explanations of phenomena that are broadly applicable or generalizable. Theories are built from **concepts**, which are generally accepted ideas, meanings, or characteristics associated with certain behaviors, events, or conditions. Theories and concepts guide scientific research, such as in medicine and space exploration, and help us understand both what we know and what we do not know. When researchers embark on a new study, they begin with a research question and choose research methods that are appropriate to answering that question. A **hypothesis**, or the predicted outcome or finding, helps guide the study. Understanding how a particular research idea or problem has been approached can help us to better grasp existing practices or think in new and innovative ways.

Worldviews are foundational to the ways we perceive and interpret our relationship to the natural world, and they also impact the ways we approach and value research/ scholarship. Many of the theories presented in this chapter derive from a **post-positivist** worldview, which focuses on cause and effect and attempts to reduce ideas into smaller more testable parts (Creswell, 2014). This worldview, often privileged in the modern, Western world, is only one way to consider phenomena. Other research paradigms that derive from different philosophical worldviews include **social constructivism**, which focuses on subjective meanings of experience and the complexity of many viewpoints, **advocacy/participatory**, which emphasizes research that includes an agenda for political/ policy reform particularly for the disenfranchised, **pragmatism**, which gives primacy to actions and consequences and emphasizes application, and **critical theory**, which refers to research conducted with the goal of social–cultural critique and change.

While it is necessary to be cautious when ascribing the human–landscape connection to evolutionary processes, this perspective forms the basis of many theories due to our extensive involvement with natural environments throughout history. For example, recent findings demonstrate that aesthetic preferences for landscapes vary based on both sex and education levels, suggesting both evolutionary and learned influences on landscapes preference (Wang and Zhao, 2017). This is in line with Mitten's (2017) contention that humans are born with an inclination to affiliate with nature, but that tendency often

DOI: 10.1079/9781789245400.0004

needs to be nurtured to fully materialize. Other theories presented here emphasize the restorative potential of natural landscapes, the importance of personal connections via identity, and other relevant psychological frameworks. This chapter provides an introduction and background information for many of these theories, concluding with practical applications.

Evolutionary-based Theories

Biophilia hypothesis

The term biophilia, meaning "love of life," was first coined by social psychologist Eric Fromm in 1964. Later popularized in the USA by E.O. Wilson (1984), and adapted to refer specifically to the relationship between humans and the natural world, the **biophilia hypothesis** theorizes that humans have an affinity to life forms, such as plants, animals, and other aspects of landscapes that stems from evolutionary and subsequent genetic processes, and therefore "prefer" or seek natural environments. Conversely, not being in close contact physical with natural environments can create feelings of dysfunction or ill health. The hypothesis contends that human identity and personal fulfillment depend on our relationship to nature, as does humans' positive emotional, cognitive, aesthetic, and spiritual development.

An underlying assumption of the biophilia hypothesis is that humans evolved for millions of years as a part of natural landscapes and developed a complex of biological innate learning rules to mediate our experiences in these environments. Kellert (2012) argued there are eight fundamental ways that humans find meaning and benefit in the natural world: attraction, reason, aversion, exploitation, affection, dominion, spirituality, and symbolism. These eight **biophilic values** represent the varied ways that humans interact with the natural environment and in each case can develop in adaptive or maladaptive ways. According to Kellert (2012), the conscious cultivation of each of these values leads to optimum human functioning and allows for an environmental ethic necessary to reverse current social and environmental crises.

Criticisms surrounding the biophilia hypothesis focus on the degree to which phenomena such as epigenetics, past experience, culture, and social learning serve to offset any effects of evolution. In addition, some contend the fact that natural landscapes represent settings that may be feared, disliked, or otherwise viewed negatively (e.g. Bixler and Floyd, 1997) argue against the development of positive attitudes toward nature. The biophilia hypothesis accounts for a measured or healthy fear of some parts of the natural world, such as snakes or heights, that is essential for humans' survival. Therefore, a balance between healthy fear of some aspects of nature and a positive affiliation with nature increases well-being and survival.

Naturalistic intelligence

Another early theory that derives from an evolutionary perspective is Gardner's **theory of multiple intelligences**, which is grounded in the work of Maria Montessori (Swiderski, 2011). This theory conceptualizes human intelligence as more than a person's cognitive ability. When first published in 1983, it included seven intelligences: linguistic, musical, logical–mathematical, spatial, bodily kinesthetic, interpersonal, and intrapersonal. Gardner (1999) later added **naturalistic intelligence** as an eighth intelligence, which refers to the ability to focus on environmental patterns and connections in natural systems. This theory has been subject to a fair amount of criticism due to lack of empirical testing and support. Still, the ideas Gardner put forth may be useful in nurturing our connection to landscapes. It makes sense that humans would have naturalistic intelligence through genetics, epigenetics, innate brain development, or other avenues because being in tune with nature would help individual and species survival (Mitten, 2017). Nurturing naturalistic intelligence can help people develop an ethic of care through being sensitive to their role in nature and through nurturing other people and the environment.

Other evolutionary-grounded theories

Several lesser known theories of human attraction to natural landscapes also have a basis in evolution. The **savannah theory** suggests that our ancestral people selected savannah-like terrain features over other landscape types because they provided sites more suitable for survival, including features such as shelter, concealment, water, and food (Orians and Heerwagen, 1992). The savannah theory posits that there exists an emotional connection between people and savannah-like landscapes. Appleton's (1990) **prospect-refuge theory** also considers habitat suitability as a mechanism to explain the attractiveness of certain landscapes and combines this with **information processing theory**—a cognitive psychology theory that uses the analogy of a computer to understand the way the human brain processes information. Critics have labeled prospect-refuge theory as reductionist, and both theories have limited supporting evidence. More recent findings suggest that familiarity with a specific type of landscape may be as important a predictor of landscape selection (Adevi and Grahn, 2012). The development and subsequent critique of these theories demonstrates the pursuit of the landscape architecture field, in particular, to better understand human aesthetic preferences and to apply that understanding in the design of landscapes.

A strength of these related theories is that they represent a number of different fields and come to comparable conclusions—that humans interact with nature in purposeful and influential ways. Doubtless, there are numerous other factors and influences that facilitate these connections, including cultural and iconic symbols, places of emotional and historical significance, and idiosyncratic events such as a budding relationship, beautiful weather, or a feeling of awe. While mere attraction to a setting does not necessarily implicate a positive health outcome, several theories specifically explore the restorative effects of natural settings.

Restorative Environment Theories

Some of the most well-known theories linking landscapes and human health focus on the restorative effects of time spent in a particular environment. **Restoration** is a process through which people recover personal resources that have been diminished through the demands of everyday life or other challenging events (Hartig, 2004). The literature in this area is dominated by two main theories that propose this type of relationship— **stress reduction theory** (SRT)[1] and **attention restoration theory** (ART).

Stress reduction theory

In developing SRT, Ulrich (1984) and colleagues (Ulrich *et al.*, 1991) observed that environmental stressors such as crowding, noise, and pollution can cause stress and wondered about the possibility of other types of environments fostering stress recovery. **Stress** can be thought of as an individual's psychological, physiological, and/or behavioral response to a situation that challenges or threatens an individual's sense of well-being and personal control (Edelstein, 2002) and has also been operationalized as the impairment of performance when the demands of a task exceeds one's available resources. Psychological effects of stress can be manifested in emotions such as fear, anger, depression, or inefficiencies in coping, whereas physiological manifestations of stress can impact the muscular, cardiovascular, or neuroendocrine systems. In reaction to stress, behavioral outcomes may include avoidance, substance abuse, and declines in cognitive and behavioral performances.

An early and influential study contributing to the development of SRT investigated the impacts of viewing nature on recovery rates of surgery patients. After observing surgery patients who either had a room with a view of nature or a room without such a view, Ulrich (1984) found that the patients with the view of nature had shorter recovery times, required less pain medication, and had lower incidents of medical issues associated with their surgery when compared with the patients without the view of nature. In a follow-up study, Ulrich *et al.* (1991) showed a stress-inducing video of workplace accidents to research subjects and then measured psychological and physiological response during a recovery period, where subjects watched videos of either natural or urban scenes. The subjects who were exposed to natural scenes recuperated faster and more completely. These early studies measured the effects of viewing scenes as a proxy for the actual experience of different environments and are foundational to later studies when newer technologies allowed for field-based research.

Based on the proposition that affect precedes cognition, SRT emphasizes emotions and the immediacy of affect or feeling. That is, because of our ancestral direct connection to natural landscapes, humans can experience immediate reactions to natural environments well before they have had a chance to analyze these environments through cognitive processes. This evolutionarily adaptive response allows for both negatively toned feelings such as fear/disgust and positively toned feelings such as attention, interest, and reduced physiological arousal/stress reduction. Stress recovery occurs in settings that evoke interest, pleasantness, and calm, which is an area where biophilia and SRT mix. Humans are attracted to natural environments, and this attraction helps reduce negative factors such as stress and promotes overall survival by predisposing humans to seek out pleasant (and safe) settings. Due to factors of evolution and the relative amount of time our species has spent immersed in natural landscapes, humans may lack this same biologically programmed response to urban or built settings; therefore, these types of settings may not (yet) offer the same opportunities for stress reduction and recovery.

This biological programming may result in a preference for certain environments, and SRT postulates that this preference chronologically occurs first, followed by cognitive awareness. Central to SRT is the belief that positive changes in perceptions and subsequent emotions such as a sense of calm or joy can be facilitated through natural landscape exposure, primarily because of evolutionary learnings and background. While SRT centers on restoration from negative emotional states, or physiological depletion of resources such as energy levels due to stress, ART emphasizes restoration as a way to improve everyday functioning through recovery from attention fatigue.

Attention restoration theory

In formulating ART, R. Kaplan and S. Kaplan (1989) posited that attention is a finite resource and once depleted, it needs to be restored in order for humans to function optimally in their environments. This idea is based on the earlier work of William James (1842–1910) regarding involuntary and voluntary attention. Involuntary attention requires almost no effort, whereas voluntary attention, later called **directed attention** by the authors of ART, requires effort, plays a central role in achieving and maintaining focus, is usually under a cognitive-control process, is important for problem solving, controls distraction through inhibition, and is susceptible to fatigue. S. Kaplan (1995) theorized that directed attention is a key resource in modern life as it aids executive functioning, our ability to be organized and purposeful, and our capacity to interact civilly with others, and yet it is fragile, often making it the "weak link" in the problem-solving chain. From an evolutionary perspective, this may have made sense as the ability to maintain focus for long periods of time would render a human vulnerable, but the modern world that humans now inhabit is full of myriad distractions that we must constantly inhibit to function effectively. Thus, the ability to restore our attention becomes paramount, and it is this process that speaks to the underlying role of natural landscapes through ART.

Restorative settings are those that allow directed attention to rest. Effective settings share four properties:

- *fascination*: engages attention effortlessly, allowing directed attention to rest;
- *being away*: is physically or conceptually different from one's usual environment;
- *extent*: is rich and coherent enough to engage the mind and promote exploration; and
- *compatibility*: implies a good fit between one's inclinations/purposes and the activities supported by the setting.

Fascination relates to the quality of certain settings or events that can attract and hold a person's interest or attention (R. Kaplan *et al.*, 1998) and can take two forms: (i) hard fascination; and (ii) soft fascination. Hard fascination refers to experiences or activities that are intense, riveting, and offer limited space or time for reflection or cognitive activity. Soft fascination involves activities or experiences that are moderate in intensity and can focus an individual's attention while allowing for reflection and cognition. Peaceful, natural settings are often thought to be good locations for experiencing soft fascination. Although necessary, fascination by itself is generally not considered sufficient for restoration, nor is it a guarantee of a restorative experience (S. Kaplan, 1995). The other three components of the model must also be present.

Being away implies achieving some psychological distance from the tasks, duties, or ongoing goals that an individual experiences in normal everyday living and that require directed attention (Hartig *et al.*, 2011). Conceptually, being away involves three components: (i) escape from unwelcome stimuli such as noise, traffic, or sense of crowding; (ii) leaving one's routine concerns or activities; and (iii) temporarily setting aside one's ongoing pursuit of goals or aspirations. Finally, being away can be either a physical phenomenon or a psychological transformation, or both (Han, 2001).

Extent refers to a setting that is rich and coherent enough that an individual can experience it either physically or psychologically without using directed attention. Thus, the individual remains fascinated and interested but without using psychological energy to focus directed attention.

Finally, compatibility refers to the match between an individual's purposes and what the environment and their own skill/knowledge base allows them to do. A compatible environment is responsive to the individual and provides useful feedback, requiring less selectivity due to fewer distracting or irrelevant possibilities (S. Kaplan, 1995). These characteristics require less directed attention, allowing the individual to act comfortably and naturally.

Natural landscapes, including aesthetic scenery, open space, the presence of water and vegetation, and other natural components, can be particularly effective in providing experiences of fascination, being away, extent, and compatibility, contributing to the facilitation of restorative outcomes (S. Kaplan, 1995).

Integrating the theories

While SRT and ART are similar in their conceptualization of natural settings as restorative environments, they differ in terms of the mechanism under study. Ulrich et al. (1991) claimed that attention is an inadequate explanation because attention plays a role in both restorative and non-restorative scenarios, such as encountering a snake. They asserted that SRT better accounts for both of these scenarios and that attention restoration is part of the stress reduction response, but because affect precedes cognition, the stress response comes first. In response, S. Kaplan (1995) agreed that stress and attention often co-occur and that a challenge of research in this area is to tease apart the potential confounding of these two variables. Kaplan asserted that attention fatigue is slower to develop and slower to recover than stress, and declines in resources (such as attention) can both cause stress and be the result of stress. Thus, it would appear that stress and attention are distinct but interacting components of restorative environment experiences. S. Kaplan (1995) proposed an integrated framework of both theories and suggested that attending to the stress–attention relationship might provide greater insight into the overall benefits of restorative environments.

Identity-based Theories

Another way of conceptualizing our connection to landscapes and understanding the related pathways to health is through the concept of identity. Authors from a variety of disciplines have characterized the sense of connection individuals experience in relation to natural settings, utilizing terms such as **place identity** (e.g. Proshansky et al., 1983; Korpela, 1989), **ecological identity** (e.g. Thomashow, 1996), and **environmental identity** (e.g. Clayton, 2003; Weigert, 2008). Clayton (2003), a psychologist, defined environmental identity as "a sense of connection to some part of the non-human natural environment, based on history, emotional attachment, and/or similarity, that affects the ways we perceive and act toward the world" (pp. 45–46). This identity serves to inform people of who they are, as well as their understanding of nature and environmental issues. Weigert (1997), a sociologist, defined environmental identity as the "experienced social understanding of who we are in relation to, and how we interact with, the natural environment as other" (p. 159). Regardless of disciplinary lens, identity informs us of who we are. In the case of environmental, ecological, and place identity, natural landscapes can influence the ways we think about ourselves and about what it means to be human (Clayton, 2003).

The dominant Western value of individualism extends to the conceptualization of selfhood. Once we escape the belief that Western ideals are universal, we begin to see other cultural conceptualizations of self with more communal or collective orientations, such as in diverse Indigenous and African self-concepts (Kretz, 2014). An ecological perception of self similarly helps to shift self-motivation toward community orientations. This emphasis on relatedness is also stressed in ecofeminist approaches (see Chapter 6, this volume).

The idea of the ecological self arises from the deep ecology movement and invokes our fundamental relatedness—not only with other humans, but with all beings (Kretz, 2014). **Deep ecology** is a philosophy that emphasizes the equal rights and intrinsic value of all nature, recognizing humans as part of nature rather than separate from or in control of natural processes (Naess, 1985). Naess (1985) defined **identification** as "a spontaneous, non-rational, but not irrational, process through which the interests of another being are reacted to as our own interest or interests" (p. 152). This process of identification with all beings—including plants, animals, and landscapes—allows for a sense of unity, the opposite of which is alienation. An important tenet of deep ecology is the importance of diversity—both in terms of species biodiversity and in terms of human cultures, economies, and ways of life. Thus, deep ecologists attend simultaneously to environmental issues and sociopolitical issues of oppression, while considering personal development and self-realization.

Kretz (2014) defined the ecological self as "relational, reflective of community relations, cooperative, and revealing a world seen through the clarifying lens of ecology" (p. 5). She argued that nurturing the ecological self provides an alternative to neoliberal selfhood in a way that reveals the limitations of dominant individualistic ideologies and promotes a sense of membership in a larger community of life. Ecological identity work is a particular practice that encourages students to understand themselves in relation to not only their perceptions of nature, but also their relevant social and political contexts (Thomashow, 1996). As an educational process, ecological identity work can promote citizenship, responsibility, critical thinking, and awareness of human–nature relationships in a way that equips students to deal with real-world problems (Kretz, 2014).

Regardless of terminology, the fundamental nature of an environmental identity, or humans' relationship with natural landscapes, is woven throughout existing research. The biophilia hypothesis, for example, asserts an inherent human *need* to affiliate with and value nature, going so far as to propose a "deprived and diminished existence" (Kellert, 1993, p. 43) for those who are unable to fulfill this need. Identity is implicated in the ways we perceive and act toward the natural world and is therefore also important in considering the health of our planet.

Australia: Indigenous teaching through stories and songlines, and from Mother Earth
By Gulaga (Mother Mountain), Lynne Thomas, and Tonia Gray

For countless decades, Indigenous peoples have warned our neoliberal capitalist society that their distinct lack of awareness of traditional Indigenous knowledge (TIK) and respect for Mother Earth creates an impending spiritual and ecological crisis. Australian Indigenous people know Mother Earth has a spirit—a natural intelligence—whose laws are based on love, relationship, reciprocal respect, kindness, and sharing. Mother Nature is our genuine teacher. Aboriginal Elder Tex Skuthorpe reveals, "Our land is our knowledge, we walk on the knowledge, we dwell in the knowledge, we live in our thesaurus, we walk in our Bible every day of our lives. Everything is knowledge." (T. Skuthorpe, New South Wales, Australia, 2017, personal communication).

Dadirri, a form of introspection and attunement to nature, is integral to Indigenous practice. Aboriginal Elder Miriam Rose Ungunmerr Baumann refers to *dadirri* or deep listening as:

To know me is to breathe with me.
To breathe with me is to listen deeply.
To listen deeply is to connect.
It is the sound of deep calling to deep.
Dadirri [is] the deep inner spring inside us.
We call on it and it calls on us.
        (The Dadirri Film Project, 2015)

To gain a sense of how things "tie together," we need to go back to Country, which holds the template of all learnings. An understanding of Country starts with the notion that Country is a nourishing terrain. Country is a place that both gives, and receives, life. Country is a living entity with a yesterday (past), a today (present), and tomorrow (future).

Aboriginal ways of knowing are based upon ancient knowledge systems that demand an intimacy with the landscape and their songlines or ley lines. Dreaming stories reconstruct Aboriginal creation stories and articulate how culture is inextricably connected to the physical, cultural, and spiritual landscape through these songlines (Birrell, 2007). According to Lynne Thomas, "I tell my stories at different locations, between these locations, we follow song lines to other locations. Stories occurred between these sacred sites. My cultural education took place informally, and was (and is) a geography of knowledge[s]."

An example is a familial tie through the landscape of Gulaga to her offspring. Gulaga, a forested ancient volcano, had two sons who remain connected to the "Mother Mountain" by their respective umbilical cords (or ley lines). Gulaga's elder son Barunguba is an island surrounded by salt water 9 km off the mainland coast and joined to Gulaga by a clear water source (umbilical cord) located 70,000 fathoms under the earth. Located at the base of Mother Mountain Gulaga, and cojoined via a crystal quartz ley line (representing a frozen umbilical cord) is Gulaga's younger son affectionately called Najunuka. Barunguba, a cultural meeting place to the Yuin people and located in the South Coast region of New South Wales, is now a protected reserve jointly managed with the Yuin people.

Indigenous knowledge systems teach us we are all interconnected. One TIK law is "You never take more from than you need in order to survive." If we do, we open ourselves to insatiable materialism and self-fueling greed. Until we change our behavior and treat Mother Earth with respect, we continue the course for our own self-destruction. Mother Earth is now answering back, like a mother would, to make us wake up, to teach us, to make us feel the calamitous damage we have inflicted. Abiding by her laws requires living a simpler and harmonious lifestyle, imbued with respect and kindness for all life—human and non-human. Part of the answer is in you; part of the answer is in me. Let's begin this now.

Landscape typical of Tasmania's West Coast in Australia. Photo courtesy of Lynne Thomas, Yuin-Biripi-Maleema custodian.

Sense of place

Another way of conceptualizing our relationship to our surroundings is through the concept of place. **Place** differs from physical space by its meaning; a location becomes a place based on our personal interactions, experiences, culture, beliefs, and values (Tuan, 2001). Cresswell (2013), a geographer, wrote: "Place is not just a thing in the world ... place is also a way of seeing, knowing and understanding the world" (p. 11).

Sense of place refers specifically to the emotional, spiritual, and symbolic aspects of places (Kaltenborn, 1997) or to the meanings and emotional bonds people form with places (Eisenhauer *et al.*, 2000). Thus, sense of place speaks to the ways places are important and meaningful to individuals, and how they are connected to sense of self, and is an important concept relative to environmental behavior. Environmental issues that are personally relevant, invoke emotion, and are connected to individuals' lives are more important and salient than those issues that seem more disconnected (Crompton and Kasser, 2009). Typically, for example, one does not personally experience the extinction of the polar bears or the hole in the ozone layer, but individuals do experience changes that occur in the places that are important to them. These changes, caused by both development and climate change, impact not just the physical places themselves but also peoples' identities and emotional bonds with those places, and may even lead to social and psychological issues including trauma, grief, and loss of livelihood and social networks (Devine-Wright, 2013). Emphasizing place can be an important part of a public health response to climate change by focusing on local exposure, bringing attention to issues in the places where people are most motivated to respond (Hess *et al.*, 2008).

While most place-based research has focused on the local, recent research has begun to explore attachments to multiple places and at different scales (Devine-Wright, 2013). For example, a person might have strong attachments to a personal garden, the city they grew up in, a cherished vacation spot, and perhaps even the planet earth. Some authors have argued that developing a global place attachment, or a sense of belonging to the larger planet, could prompt necessary human response to climate change (Devine-Wright, 2013).

Sense of place has implications for both human well-being and planetary health, provides a linkage between social and ecological issues, and may even be thought of as an ecosystem service (Hausmann *et al.*, 2016). **Ecosystem services** are the benefits people receive from ecosystems, which are dependent on biodiversity and which sustain not only human health but that of all species. Thinking of sense of place in this way may help bridge existing gaps between conservation efforts and the needs and values of people in communities. This is a more transactional approach—even going so far as to assign economic value to sense of place in some cases. While this does not offset dominant worldviews and profit-driven motives, it may help encourage policy makers to consider human attachment to place as we mobilize both local and global responses to climate change.

Other Psychological Theories and Concepts

A number of theories have emerged from the field of psychology that emphasize positive emotions and a sense of connectedness with one's environment. While none of these theories refer solely to experiences in natural landscapes, experiences of the natural world may be considered prototypical to each phenomenon.

Awe refers to feelings of wonder and amazement and is often brought on by exposure to vast stimuli that "transcend current frames of reference" (Piff *et al.*, 2015, p. 884). Piff and colleagues referred to nature-based experiences as the "prototypical awe experience" in Western cultures, invoking images of the vast night sky, the ocean, and sweeping panoramic views. Awe can also arise through exposure to artwork, architecture, and other forms of beauty. Experiences of awe have been linked to feeling like one is part of something larger, or a metaphorical smallness of self (Shiota *et al.*, 2007). Many of the defining characteristics of awe are also foundational to Maslow's (1964) **peak experience**, defined as joyous and exciting moments involving intense feelings of well-being, wonder, and/or awe. Peak experiences often come on suddenly and are inspired by meditation, reflection, or the overwhelming beauty of nature. They can become permanent features in an individual's memory and can be therapeutic by increasing a sense of self-determination, creativity, and empathy.

Research indicates that these types of experiences can lead individuals to focus less on personal concerns and attend more to prosocial behaviors relative to the larger collective (Piff *et al.*, 2015). While much of the existing research emphasizes experiences of grandeur, Ballew and Omoto (2018) demonstrated that even short, relatively mundane nature experiences can produce feelings of awe if individuals are able to achieve a sense of absorption in their environments—a key idea connecting awe, ART, mindfulness, and the theory of **flow**.

Originally proposed by Csikszentmihalyi (1975), flow can be defined as a mental state in which a person is engaged in single-minded immersion while performing an activity and experiencing feelings of joy, deep focus, and absorption. Csikszentmihalyi (1997) suggested flow can be linked to a balance between the challenge an individual faces and the skill level they possess. Encounters with nature often provide many of the prerequisite factors of flow, such as intense focus, loss of the temporal experience, or a merging of action and personal awareness. The innately fascinating characteristics of nature are likely to promote this sense of total absorption and captivation with one's surroundings (Ballew and Omoto, 2018).

Conclusion

Scientific findings and associated theories represent an ongoing conversation among researchers, who are constantly striving to test one another's ideas to learn and discover more. This iterative process can be seen in this chapter in the ongoing critiques between the authors of ART, SRT and biophilia, as well as between authors from various disciplines writing about identity. Collectively, these ideas serve to inform our thinking about the impact of our immediate surroundings on our well-being. Some of these theories approach this idea from an evolutionary perspective, while others focus more on an individual's cognition or sense of self. Still others utilize a combination of approaches, weaving a multifaceted explanation for the importance of the natural world.

As humans, we are part of the earth and have a sense of longing, connection, and remembrance of being outdoors that can be sparked through nurturance. Through the study of epigenetics, we know that humans have memory at the cellular level that is passed down through generations. As a species, we have over 30,000 generations of ancestors who lived primarily outdoors, as opposed to fewer than 15 generations who have lived indoor lifestyles similar to our own. The memory and the sense of connection to the natural world are ingrained in our bodies.

The ideas presented in this chapter arise from different ways of thinking about or explaining this phenomenon, using a particular language and worldview. A strength of the research paradigm is that it enables scientists and researchers to communicate about this engrained bodily knowledge and integrate it into ongoing theory and practice in disciplines such as medicine, public health, planning, and education that impact our day-to-day lives. Slowly but surely, Western scientific research has begun to accept other worldviews and ideas, and this diversity of thought provides greater understanding of the world around us. Much of the research presented in the next chapter builds on the foundation of the theories presented here.

Note

[1] Also sometimes referred to as psychoevolutionary theory, which is distinct from Plutchik's (1980) psychoevolutionary theory of emotions.

References

Adevi, A. and Grahn, P. (2012) Preferences for landscapes: a matter of cultural determinants or innate reflexes that point to our evolutionary background? *Landscape Research* 37(1), 27–49.

Appleton, J. (1990) *The Symbolism of Habitat: an Interpretation of Landscape in the Arts.* University of Washington Press, Seattle, State of Washington.

Ballew, M. and Omoto, A. (2018) Absorption: how nature experiences promote awe and other positive emotions. *Ecopsychology* 10(1), 26–35.

Bickman, L. and Rog, D. (2009) *The SAGE Handbook of Applied Social Science.* SAGE Publications, Newbury, New Jersey.

Birrell, C.L. (2007) Meeting country: a deep engagement with place and Indigenous culture. Doctoral thesis, University of Western Sydney, Sydney, Australia. Available at: http://researchdirect.uws.edu.au/islandora/object/uws%3A2519/datastream/PDF/download/citation.pdf (accessed 24 December 2020).

Bixler, R. and Floyd, M. (1997) Nature is scary, disgusting, and uncomfortable. *Environment and Behavior* 29(4), 17–22.

Clayton, S. (2003) *Environmental Identity: a Conceptual and Operational Definition.* MIT Press, Cambridge, Massachusetts.

Creswell, J. (2014) The selection of a research approach. In: *Research Design: Qualitative, Quantitative, and Mixed Methods Approaches.* Sage Publications, Thousand Oaks, California, pp. 3–24.

Cresswell, T. (2013) *Place: a Short Introduction.* Wiley, Malden, Massachusetts.

Crompton, T. and Kasser, T. (2009) *Meeting Environmental Challenges: the Role of Human Identity.* WWF-UK, Godalming, UK.

Csikszentmihalyi, M. (1975) *Beyond Boredom and Anxiety: the Experience of Play in Work and Games.* Jossey-Bass, San Francisco, California.

Csikszentmihalyi, M. (1997) *Finding Flow: the Psychology of Engagement with Everyday Life.* Basic Books, New York.

Devine-Wright, P. (2013) Think global, act local? The relevance of place attachments and place identities in a climate changed world. *Global Environmental Change* 23(1), 61–69.

Edelstein, M.R. (2002) Contamination: the invisible built environment. In: Bechtel, R. and Churchman, A. (eds) *Handbook of Environmental Psychology.* Wiley, New York, pp. 567–570.

Eisenhauer, B., Krannich, R. and Blahna, D. (2000) Attachments to special places on public lands: an analysis of activities, reason for attachments, and community connections. *Society & Natural Resources* 13(5), 421–441.

Gardner, H. (1999) *Intelligence Reframed: Multiple Intelligences for the 21st Century.* Basic Books, New York.

Han, K. (2001) A review: theories of restorative environments. *Journal of Therapeutic Horticulture* 12, 30–43.

Hartig, T. (2004) Restorative environments. In: Spielberger, C. (ed.) *Encyclopedia of Applied Psychology.* Academic Press, San Diego, California, pp. 273–279.

Hartig, T., van den Berg, A., Hagerhall, C., Tomalak, M., Bauer, N., *et al.* (2011) Health benefits and nature experiences: psychological, social and cultural processes. In: Nilsson, K.,

Sangster, M., Gallis, C., Hartig, T., de Vries, S., *et al.* (eds) *Forests, Trees and Human Health.* Springer, New York, pp. 127–168.

Hausmann, A., Slotow, R., Burns, J. and Di Minin, E. (2016) The ecosystem service of sense of place: benefits for human well-being and biodiversity conservation. *Environmental Conservation* 43(2), 117–127.

Hess, J., Malilay, J. and Parkinson, A. (2008) Climate change: the importance of place. *American Journal of Preventive Medicine* 35(5), 468–478.

Kaltenborn, B. (1997) Nature of place attachment: a study among recreation homeowners in southern Norway. *Leisure Sciences* 19(3), 175–189.

Kaplan, R. and Kaplan, S. (1989) *The Experience of Nature: a Psychological Perspective.* Cambridge University Press, Cambridge, Massachusetts.

Kaplan, R., Kaplan, S. and Ryan, R. (1998) *With People in Mind: Design and Management of Everyday Nature.* Island Press, Washington, DC.

Kaplan, S. (1995) The restorative benefits of nature: toward an integrative framework. *Journal of Environmental Psychology* 15(3), 169–182.

Kellert, S.R. (1993) The biological basis for human values of nature. In: *The Biophilia Hypothesis.* Island Press, Washington, DC, pp. 42–69.

Kellert, S. (2012) *Birthright: People and Nature in the Modern World.* Yale University Press, New Haven, Connecticut.

Korpela, K. (1989) Place-identity as a product of environmental self-regulation. *Journal of Environmental Psychology* 9(3), 241–256.

Kretz, L. (2014) Ecological identity in education: subverting the neoliberal self. *Leadership and Research in Education* 1, 4–21.

Maslow, A. (1964) *Religion, Values, and Peak-Experiences.* The Ohio State University Press, Columbus, Ohio.

Mitten, D. (2017) Connections, compassion and co-healing: the ecology of relationship. In: Malone, K., Truong, S. and Gray, T. (eds) *Reimagining Sustainability in Precarious Times.* Springer Science+Business Media, Singapore, pp. 173–186.

Naess, A. (1985) Identification as a source of deep ecological attitudes. Reprinted in: Pojman, L.P. (ed.) *Environmental Ethics: Readings in Theory and Application.* Wadsworth, Belmont, California, pp. 150–157.

Orians, G. and Heerwagen, J. (1992) Evolved responses to landscapes. In: Barlow, J.H., Cosmides, L. and Tooby, J. (eds) *The Adapted Mind, Evolutionary Psychology and the Generation of Culture.* Oxford University Press, New York, pp. 555–581.

Piff, P., Dietze, P., Feinberg, M., Stancato, D. and Keltner, D. (2015) Awe, the small self, and prosocial behavior. *Journal of Personality and Social Psychology* 108(6), 883.

Plutchik, R. (1980) A general psychoevolutionary theory of emotion. In: Plutchik, R. and Kellerman, H. (eds) *Emotion: Theory, Research, and Experience: Vol. 1. Theories of Emotion.* Academic Press, New York, pp. 3–33.

Proshansky, H., Fabian, A. and Kaminoff, R. (1983) Place-identity: physical world socialization of the self. *Journal of Environmental Psychology* 3(1), 57–83.

Shiota, M., Keltner, D. and Mossman, A. (2007) The nature of awe: elicitors, appraisals, and effects on self-concept. *Cognition and Emotion* 21(5), 944–963.

Swiderski, M. (2011) Maria Montessori. In: Smith, T. and Knapp, C. (eds) *Sourcebook of Experiential Education: Key Thinkers and their Contributions.* Routledge, New York, pp. 197–207.

The Dadirri Film Project (2015) DADIRRI (Official Miriam Rose Ungunmerr Baumann video). Short promotional film about Dadirri – a Gift to the Nation. Miriam Rose Foundation, Daly River, Northern Territory, Australia. Available at: https://www.youtube.com/watch?v=pkY1dGk-LyE (accessed 2 January 2021).

Thomashow, M. (1996) *Ecological Identity: Becoming a Reflective Environmentalist.* MIT Press, Cambridge, Massachusetts.

Tuan, Y. (2001) *Space and Place: the Perspective of Experience.* University of Minnesota Press, Minneapolis, Minnesota.

Ulrich, R. (1984) View through a window may influence recovery from surgery. *Science* 224(4647), 420–421.

Ulrich, R., Simons, R., Losito, B., Fiorito, E., Miles, M., *et al.* (1991) Stress recovery during exposure to natural and urban environments. *Journal of Environmental Psychology* 11, 201–230.

Wang, R. and Zhao, J. (2017) Demographic groups' differences in visual preference for vegetated landscapes in urban green space. *Sustainable Cities and Society* 28, 350–357.

Weigert, A.J. (1997) *Self, Interaction, and Natural Environment: Refocusing Our Eyesight.* SUNY Press, Albany, New York.

Weigert, A. (2008) Pragmatic thinking about self, society, and natural environment: Mead, Carson, and beyond. *Symbolic Interaction* 31(3), 235–258.

Wilson, E.O. (1984) *Biophilia: the Human Bond with Other Species*. Harvard University Press, Cambridge, Massachusetts.

5 Outcomes, Benefits, and Opportunities: Western Research Trends

> Human-centredness is a complex syndrome which includes the hyperseparation of humans as a special species and the reduction of non-humans to their usefulness to humans, or instrumentalism. Many have claimed that this is the only prudent, rational or possible course. I argue contrary to this that human-centredness is not in the interests of either humans or non-humans, that it is even dangerous and irrational.
>
> ~Val Plumwood, PhD, ecofeminist and environmental philosopher

Throughout history, many cultures have recognized the salutogenic value of green and blue landscapes. Modern researchers study specific health benefits that humans receive from various engagements with natural landscapes, as well as the causal mechanisms for transmission, and they wonder how to mitigate effects the current estrangement (see Chapter 2, this volume) from natural landscapes has on society and individuals' physical, emotional, cognitive, and spiritual well-being.

Through millennia, humans have incidentally and intentionally interacted with landscapes in ways that benefit our health, defined as well-being, through preventing, healing, or curing maladies. For over 60,000 years, healers from many traditions have worked with nature to learn specific remedies and practices (e.g. herbalist, Chinese, and Kampo medicine; see Chapter 2, this volume). To **cure** is to eradicate a disease condition or symptom(s) that the patient has, which happens at the level of the body. However, there are times when curing a disease or disorder is not possible, such as terminal cancer or the effects of trauma or abuse. In these cases, natural landscapes can be spaces for **healing**—a process that leads to a sense of well-being and happens to the whole person. People describe this sense of well-being as joy, serenity, optimism, and confidence and trust in life. For example, watching a sunset or a calm body of water can result in healing.

Numerous Western-trained researchers and healthcare workers have long been interested in the preventive, healing, and curative effects of nature. Coming from a mechanical view of interactions, they have primarily focused on using bits of nature to cure specific ailments. For example, chemicals taken from foxglove (*Digitalis lanata*) are used to make a prescription drug for congestive heart failure called digoxin. The bark of some willows (e.g. black willow (*Salix nigra*) and white willow (*Salix alba*)) contain salicin and has been used for over 3500 years to relieve pain, inflammation, and fever. In the 1800s, aspirin was synthesized from salicin and continues to be the most widely used clinical drug worldwide (Montinari *et al.*, 2019). Component parts of nature are useful for health and healing, but a systems-focused approach, such as socioecological solutions, makes sense for both human and planetary well-being.

This chapter presents some of the research outcomes connecting human well-being and landscapes and explores the complexities inherent in the development of a field of study. In learning more about the research, we encourage readers to keep in mind:

- A primary goal of researching landscapes and human interactions is to help us discover more about creating or maintaining mutually beneficial relationships between humans and natural landscapes based on an understanding that the two are entwined.

DOI: 10.1079/9781789245400.0005

- It is less expensive (financially, psychologically, and socially) to keep people healthy than to have people regain their health. If nature is accessible and helps people stay healthy, there are positive financial implications for healthcare.
- Studying human interactions with landscapes through a systems approach is required to successfully operationalize and apply research to address well-being concerns equitably and globally. Socioecological research-based solutions consider a system of well-being incorporating both human health and environmental health (discussed more in Chapter 7, this volume).
- The positive health benefits of exposure to land and seascapes on human systems are not accessible to all populations because of economic disparities, location, and health conditions.
- Globally, nature and human well-being relationship findings have useful implications for individual well-being, public health, and landscape design.

Exposure to Nature Increases Human Well-being

In recent decades, Western researchers have made significant advances in fields of study related to natural landscapes and well-being, strengthening findings as well as uncovering greater complexities, confirming that spending time in unpolluted nature (see Chapter 3, this volume), viewing simulated nature scenes, being exposed to foliage and flowers indoors, or developing urban green spaces in large metropolitan areas are all approaches that help prevent, cure, and heal human maladies as well as lead to healthier and more mutualistic relationships with natural landscapes. Interaction with natural landscapes, including through participation in physical activity, restoration of mental and emotional health, and time with social contacts—even simply viewing or being in nature—all have a role in mental, emotional, physical, and spiritual well-being. This has prompted detailed cross-sectional, retrospective, and prospective studies examining individual and public health benefits including those potentially provided by integrating spaces with high biodiversity in urban areas.

A plethora of settings and outcome measures have been explored in varying depth and complexity, as represented by Figures 5.1 and 5.2, respectively. Figure 5.3 displays many of the research-supported outcomes of spending time in or viewing nature. Because conditions vary for each individual research study, we cannot say definitively that these benefits will happen for every person or in every instance, but the overall breadth of research helps us to be confident in the primary assertion that exposure to natural landscapes can be beneficial to human health. Building on the studies that comprise this list, future studies can help improve confidence levels in the results and help us to better understand necessary conditions and demographic variations.

Developing a Body of Knowledge

Research comes from the obsolete French *recerche*, which meant "to search carefully" or "to search again and again." As exciting as it may be that nature appears to be beneficial in myriad ways, a handful of studies demonstrating correlation or statistical significance are not conclusive. However, studies build on each other, becoming more sophisticated in terms of questions asked and methods employed and as new technology becomes available for measuring results. Over time, gaps in knowledge are identified and resolved facilitating the production of more conclusive and nuanced

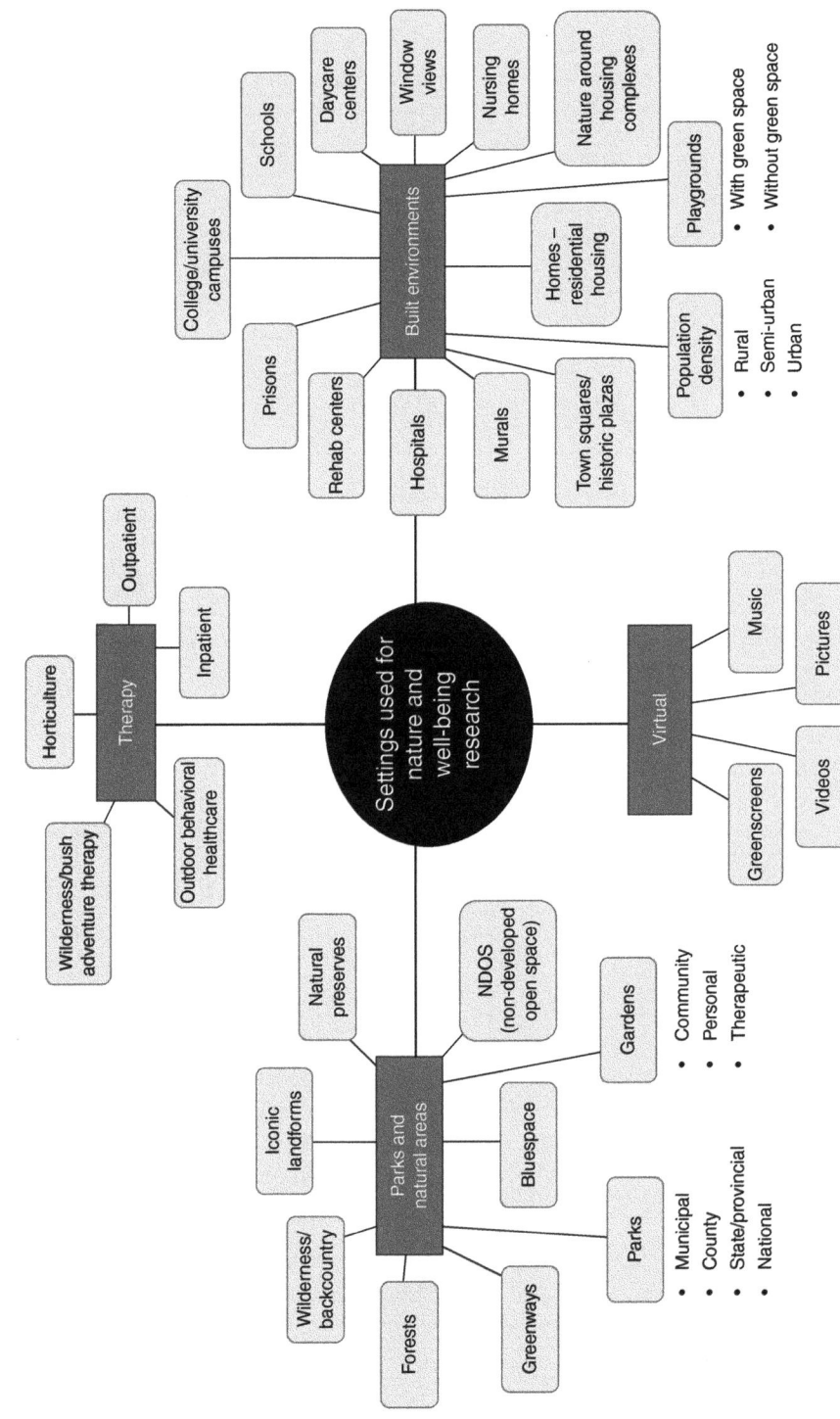

Fig. 5.1. Many outdoor, indoor, and virtual settings have been studied related to nature and well-being.

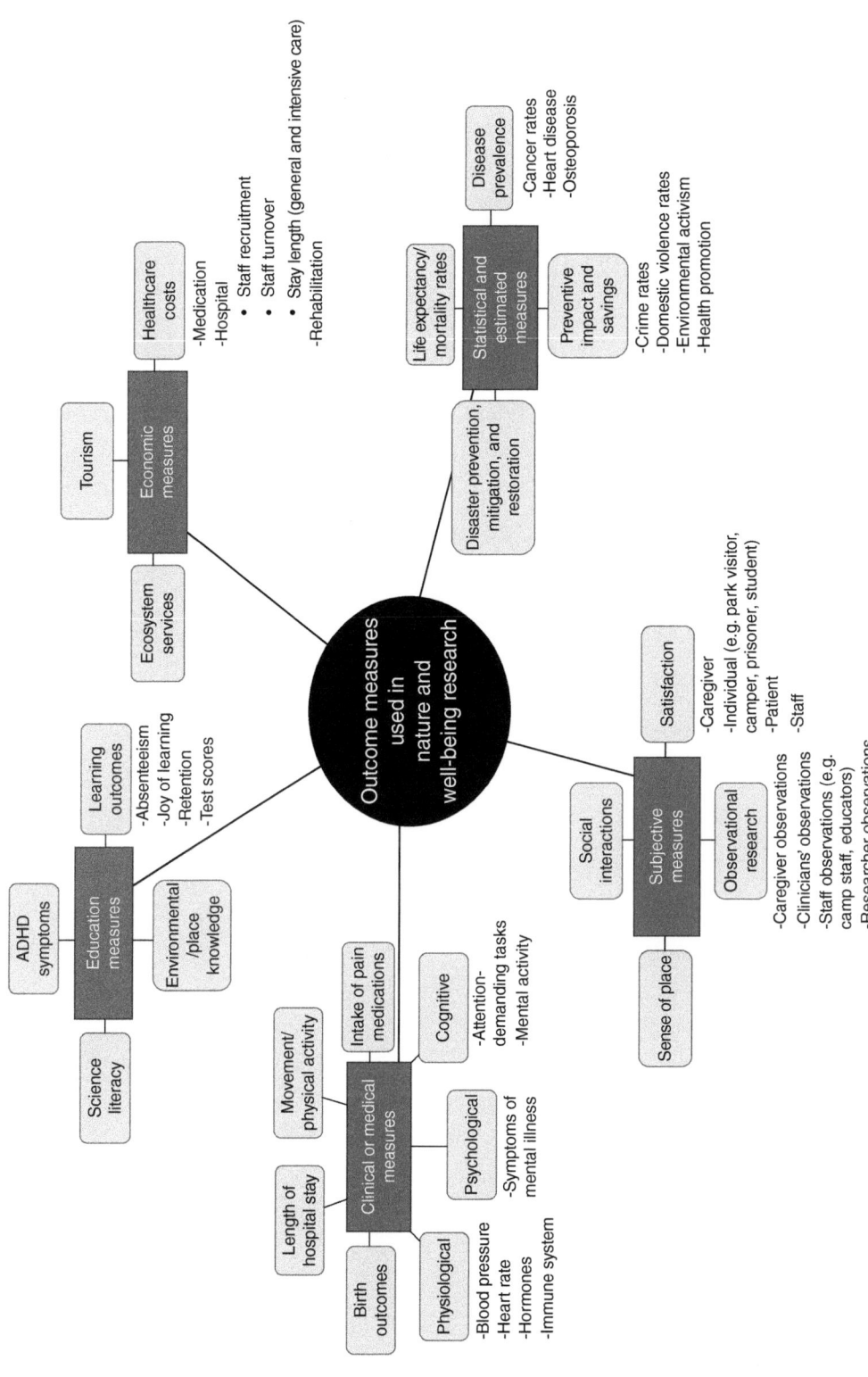

Fig. 5.2. Many outcome measures are used in nature and well-being research.

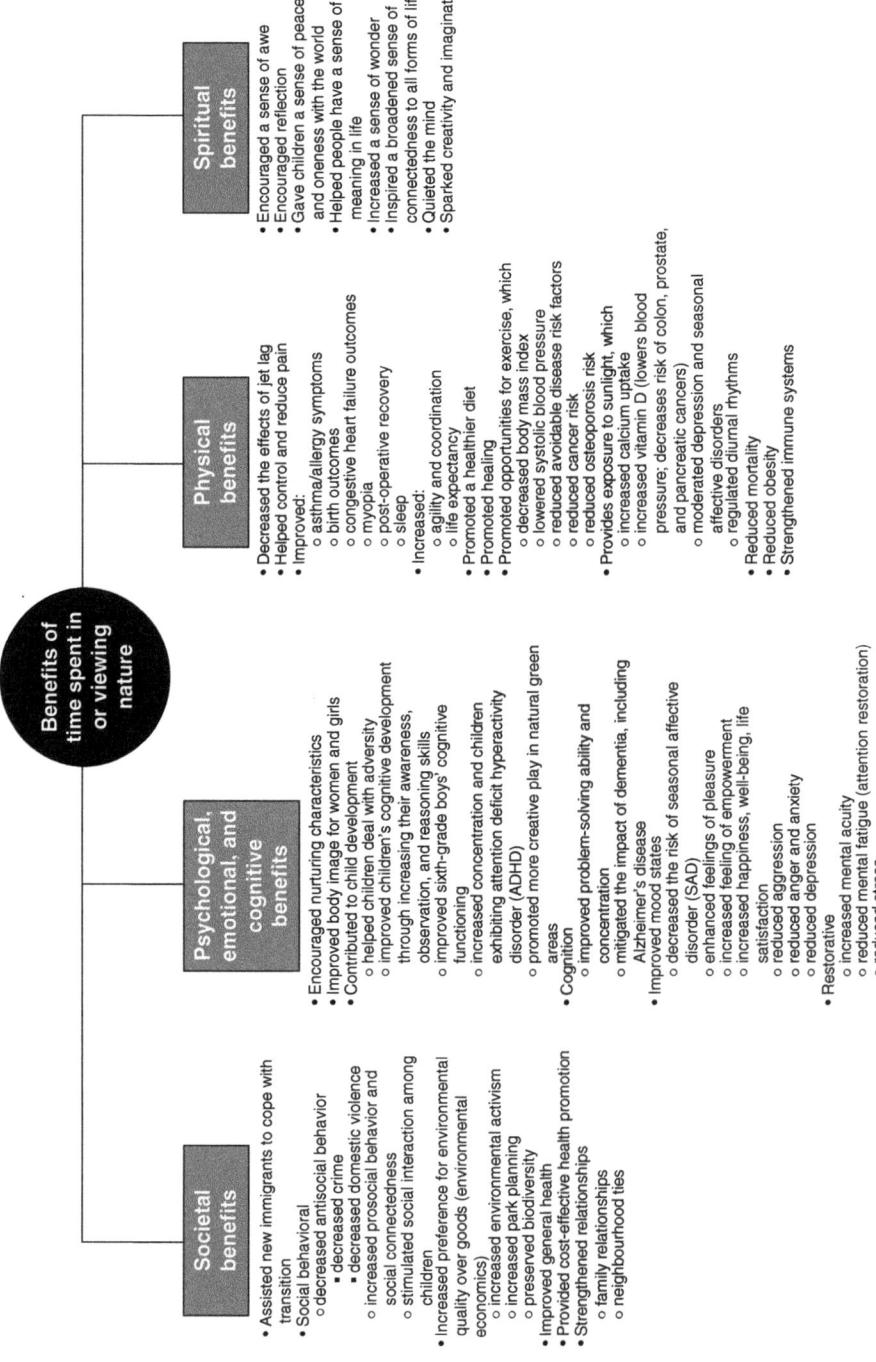

Figure 5.3. Research has reported many benefits from exposure to landscapes that can potentially be garnered by society and individuals in physical, psychological, emotional, cognitive, and spiritual domains.

information. Finally, enough peer-reviewed articles are available to conduct various reviews of the body of literature to continue the cycle of improving methods, finding gaps, and searching again.

As an example, restoration research linking landscapes and human well-being jumped forward with Ulrich's (1984) retrospective study that found patients' views from their hospital windows impacted the speed and comfort of their recovery from surgery. This study was key to developing the theory that landscapes can influence a patient's emotional state, which might then affect recovery. Ulrich's work creatively combined and built on 1970s' research from the fields of psychology, outdoor recreation, and landscape research, which suggested that US and European groups preferred viewing natural scenes—especially scenes with water—over urban scenes.

Building on the work of Ulrich and others, studies using self-reported emotional states and measuring physiological responses, including clinical measures such as heart-rate metrics, differences in hormone levels and endocrine function, and blood pressure concluded that most natural views and immersion in natural landscapes elicit positive emotions, reduce fear in stressed subjects, and hold interest. These positive changes were thought to relate to potential restorative effects of nature from anxiety or stress and short-term recovery from mental fatigue (see Chapter 4, this volume).

As a body of knowledge develops and knowledge is shared through peer-reviewed journals and other means researchers discover gaps in the knowledge, previously over-looked connections, and biased methodology that may have been applied.

Identifying and addressing research critiques

Velarde *et al.* (2007) drew attention to the fact that early research about aesthetic and affective responses to visual and immersion environments only used broad categories of natural or urban. While this dichotomy between natural and urban landscapes helped set up experimental conditions with enough contrast in views to elicit significantly different responses and likely helped researchers develop valid measures of restoration (Scopelliti *et al.*, 2019), the specific views chosen for each category could lead to confirmation bias—for example, busy streets to represent urban environments and sublime recreation/leisure areas to represent natural landscapes (Staats *et al.*, 2016).

Chiang *et al.* (2017) responded, finding that vegetation type and density played important roles in the physiological and psychological responses of individuals and that view features such as **coherence** (the ability to easily comprehend or organize a scene), **prospect** (the overall viewshed), and **refuge** (opportunities for cover) were more important than strict delineations between natural/urban or vegetation/no vegetation. Van Esch *et al.* (2019) found that overall features of a view better predicted psychological, physical, and job-specific well-being than the overall amount of nature in a view, and that certain built features could positively influence well-being. They found that people were uncomfortable with incoherent, illegible, and busy views—in both natural and built settings. Van den Berg *et al.* (2016) added to this notion of visual complexity, utilizing fractal geometry to see if fractal complexity influenced restorative values for people. They found that fractal-like, recursive complexity—different than illegible busyness—is an important visual cue underlying the restorative potential of natural and built environments.

Broadening the research

Most of the world's population now lives in urban areas; therefore, it is important that public open spaces, squares, and even small parks in urban areas, often emblematic places in cities accessible to many urban dwellers, are being considered by researchers. Scopelliti *et al.* (2019) found that an historical plaza in Rome rated as high as urban green space in its perceived restoration value. Subiza-Pérez *et al.* (2019) also investigated public squares, concluding that theories of restoration should be extended to encompass the study of built and mixed urban environments. After visiting an urban square, students reported reduced anger, hostility, tension, anxiety, fatigue, and stress, along with increased happiness, though San Juan *et al.* (2017) did not find that greenness was a factor in the restorative effect, suggesting that restoration in built environments may be processed differently from that in natural landscapes. When comparing an historical, mostly built, urban environment to a forest, Stigsdotter *et al.* (2017) found neither had measurable physiological effects (on heart-rate variability or blood pressure), though the forest was assessed (self-report) with a higher perceived restorative value.

Research expanded to explore the effects of attachment to and familiarity with landscapes as well as the effect of demographic variables in relation to the well-being effect of landscapes. When people feel attached to their landscapes, the loss of landforms may impact their well-being (Satariano and Gauci, 2019). The iconic sea arch, the Azure Window in Dwejra, Gozo, lost in a sudden event in 2017, provided evidence about how a public landform may evoke both collective emotions and personal memories. Self-report studies, media coverage, and social media indicated that people experienced strong feelings of loss and grief. That particular event reawakened a collective desire to be in contact with natural landscapes and brought forth calls for more preservation and protection of these dynamic landforms, fueling the debate about whether to accept and respect the inevitable cycles of landform change or, alternatively, to resort to invasive measures to arrest or slow down such inexorable natural changes.

Attachment to iconic landforms may be due, in part, to familiarity. For older adults, Tilley *et al.* (2017) found landscape familiarity promoted positive mood aspects by triggering past positive memories. By contrast, in a survey of Spanish and Italian urban dwellers, Hidalgo *et al.* (2006) found no influence of familiarity (measured in years spent in the city) on residents' aesthetic perception of their environments. Discrepancies in research outcomes are usual and help guide future investigations.

Other nuanced research includes that of Wang and Zhao (2017) whose participants preferred heterogeneous natural landscapes, while very open or very closed homogenous landscapes had the lowest preference ratings. Looking at the effects of demographics including gender, age, living environment during childhood, and education level on the landscape preference, they found that education level and gender of respondents significantly influenced landscape preference.

Examining demographics such as gender and race can uncover potential concerns and surprises. Rosa *et al.* (2020) studying Brazilian and US students found that gender relationships to outdoor environments seem to transcend geographical and cultural contexts. They found that while women reported stronger connections to nature and tended to state that they preferred outdoor environments in which to take recreation, they were less likely than men to actually engage in nature-based recreation. Contrary to previously published assumptions, Taylor (2018) sampled college students of different races finding that Black students, like most White, preferred natural landscapes more than urban settings and reported the first thing they thought about when asked about nature was trees, forest, and plants. No respondent reported a generalized fear of nature. Taylor called for future landscape preference research to use large samples to further investigate the intersection of influences of race, gender, age, class, and educational attainment.

Synthesizing evidence

An indicator of maturation or research progress is having a sufficient body of research that one can find review articles, including state-of-the-art reviews, scoping studies, systematic reviews, and meta-analyses in academic databases, that help describe and evaluate existing findings, limitations, gaps, and possible future directions. Some reviews address general areas while others focus on a narrow topic. Examples are Baxter and Pelletier (2019) who examined the extant literature using the question "Is nature relatedness a basic human psychological need?" and Donovan *et al.* (2019) using the question "Is there a relationship between improved birth outcomes and natural landscapes?." They reported that birth outcomes is one of the most studied greenness-and-health relationships.

All types of reviews require detailed documentation of the process and are key in furthering research. **State-of-the-art reviews**, reporting the current highest level (cutting or leading edge) of development of a scientific field (or a device or technique), can stand alone or be part of other reviews. **Scoping studies**, sometimes called scoping reviews, help systematically map the literature available on a topic, identifying key concepts, theories, sources of evidence, and gaps in the research. Evidence across a range of study designs can be used; scoping reviews are not as pointed and methodical as a systematic review.

A **systematic review** identifies and reviews the evidence on a specific question within a topic using explicit, systematic, and reproducible methods. Relevant primary research is identified, selected, and critically appraised to synthesize the evidence for the review. These reviews help establish the state-of-the-art status of particular research areas and are used in meta-analyses. A **meta-analysis** combines the results of multiple studies with like methods that ask the same research question. By combining data and using statistical analysis, the meta-analysis is expected to have less degree of error than each individual study, thus providing a stronger denial or confirmation of findings.

For example, Moeller *et al.* (2018) used a scoping review based on research with care homes, inpatient wards, women's shelters, and prisons and found that nature-based interventions likely would aid many populations in full-time care or rehabilitation settings. They specifically examined virtual-reality-based simulations of natural environments, care farming, gardening/therapeutic horticulture, and animal-assisted therapies. They used peer-reviewed articles and reported their methodology—including systematic searches of eight databases—to gather 85 studies for inclusion. In addition to making applied recommendations, Moeller *et al.* (2018) assessed that there were sufficient data available to perform more detailed systematic reviews and offer further recommendations.

An example of a systematic review is Browning *et al.* (2020a) who reviewed the effects of exposure to simulated natural landscapes on human health and cognitive performance, confirming that positive mood changes occur. Also see Browning *et al.*'s (2020b) systematic review responding to a current question: "Do virtual nature experiences offer the same restoration benefits as actual time in nature?" They used a pooled sample of participants from six studies meeting the criterion of using the standardized instrument (the Positive and Negative Affect Schedule (PANAS)) before and after exposure to measure mood, and determined that positive affect (experiencing positive emotions such as joy, enthusiasm, determination, attention, and feeling inspired) increased in actual natural settings and decreased in simulated nature settings. They also noted that negative affect (emotional distress such as anxiety, sadness, or fear) decreased in both settings. They called for more research citing the small number of studies available meeting their inclusion requirements.

Researchers rely on reviews to understand the current state of a field and to develop research agendas. Below, an in-depth example demonstrates how forest-bathing research blossomed, by using systematic reviews and other pooling methods to hone findings and broaden applications.

Forest-bathing research examined

Forest bathing, a concept named *shinrin-yoku* in Japan in 1982, roughly translates to "taking in the forest atmosphere." In October 2020, close to 3000 results appeared in Google Scholar with "forest bathing" as a search term. The earliest article about forest bathing appearing in Google Scholar is from 1990, and there are only 19 articles from before 2001, displaying how quickly research in this area accelerated.

While the benefits obtained from time spent in nature are frequently linked with the increased physical activity associated with time spent outdoors, the *shinrin-yoku* literature contends that being exposed to nature in other sensory ways (e.g. seeing, hearing, smelling, and touching) has clear benefits. Benefits found by simply spending time in forests, or "forest bathing" include: (i) decreased systolic blood pressure; (ii) decreased stress levels (measured through prefrontal cortex activity and salivary cortisol); (iii) deactivated sympathetic nervous system (measured via urinary adrenaline and noradrenaline levels); and (iv) strengthened immune system (measured via enhanced natural killer cell activity and intercellular anticancer proteins). These effects may persist over time, lasting as long as 1 week after a forest-bathing session. An individual study is not confirmatory. Because most forest-bathing studies measure the same things, including blood pressure (diastolic and systolic), pulse rate, and cortisol levels (blood and saliva) of people as they engage in forest bathing they can be evaluated as a group.

Evaluating these past studies in a systematic review, Ideno *et al.* (2017) confirmed the significant effect of *shinrin-yoku* on reduction of blood pressure. On the other hand, Bach Pagès *et al.* (2020) found in their systematic review that the variable of forest type in these studies typically is not well described. This limitation, in those authors' opinions, makes definitive conclusions with respect to data patterns premature due to this high heterogeneity in the studies and the lack of consistent relationships between forest type and health variables (blood pressure, pulse rate, and cortisol levels) in the existing literature.

In two state-of-the-art reviews, Hansen *et al.* (2017) and Hansen and Jones (2020) examined the physiological and psychological effects of *shinrin-yoku* in transcontinental Japan and China. Their in-depth reviews supported that valid and reliable psychometrics had been implemented, as well as valid and reliable physiological measurements. Thus, the significant and potentially healing and health-promoting effects (e.g. stress reduction and increased holistic well-being) were recognized. They noted a dearth of scientific research conducted in Western populations and encouraged longitudinal research. They characterized forest bathing as a complementary modality, like Berger (2020) and Naor and Mayseless (2020) who encouraged the integration of nature therapy frameworks in the areas of stress reduction and life balance for healthcare professionals and students.

Forest-bathing research demonstrates advances in understanding the mechanisms of healing. Spending time in forests appears to enhance the immune response of natural killer cells, thus activating natural killer cells in humans (Tsao *et al.*, 2018), in part due to breathing the phytoncides or antimicrobial allelochemical volatile organic compounds released by the plants. However, Antonelli *et al.*'s (2020) state-of-the-art review concluded that benefits from forest bathing "cannot be solely attributed to volatile organic compounds (VOC) inhalation" (p. 23). Using Franco *et al.*'s (2017) earlier review, they concluded that there was an integrated stimulation of the five senses. They noted that most VOC inhalation research so far has been laboratory based, and that an area's tree composition can markedly influence the concentration of specific VOCs in the forest air, which also exhibits cyclic diurnal variations. Therefore, further rigorous clinical and environmental pharmacokinetic studies ought to be performed in the field.

Some companies (e.g. Qwell; Phytoncide Japan Co., Ltd) now grind up cypress trees, supposedly extracting the phytoncides, and sell the scent in a spray can for people to use in their homes and offices, or the chips to put in pillows (hinoki cypress phytoncide) as a way to relax and relieve stress and fatigue. This sort of capitalizing on and using the environment is not supported by the research and causes unnecessary environmental damage.

Taiwan: Forest therapy is an antidote to the diseases of civilization
By Guan-Jang Wu

Traditionally, Taiwanese people enjoy taking two types of "bathing" in nature for its therapeutic benefits: (i) forest bathing; and (ii) hot-spring bathing. A forest-bathing trip is a short leisure visit to a forest for relaxation and associated health benefits. It is regarded as being very similar to natural aromatherapy. In that sense, people believe that by immersing in nature and taking in the fresh air—rich in phytoncide—a whole range of benefits can be achieved in promoting physical, psychological, social, and emotional wellness.

A forest-bathing trip often involves visiting a forest for relaxation and recreation purposes. By immersing ourselves in pure and organic substances and breathing in fresh air derived from trees and dense vegetation, we can lower our stress levels and feel at ease immediately. Numerous research studies and anecdotal experiences demonstrate that the scents of trees, sounds of brooks and streams, and the feel of warmth from sunshine through forest leaves can have a calming effect on people. Particularly, recent studies have shown that forest bathing may strengthen the immune system, lower blood pressure, and have other positive effects as discussed here in Chapter 5, this volume. As people suffer from diseases of civilization and an aging society, forest therapy may be an effective way for individuals to live a healthier and longer life by reconnecting with nature.

Recently, the concept and practice of forest bathing has gained popularity and transformed into a more scholarly pursuit. The concept of forest therapy has gained support from the Taiwan Forestry Bureau, which provides areas for activity and funding for research. To advance this new field, the forest-bathing idea has taken on a more complex form than just "a walk in the woods." For instance, for a more structured experience, people can join trained guides for a meditative half-day ecotherapy excursion for relaxation and rejuvenation. Additionally, a typical forest therapy program may include practicing moving meditations, solo practices, a deep rest *yoga nidra*, self-massage, and other similar activities.

Continued

Even though the notion of forest bathing might seem novel, incorporating forest-bathing trips (i.e. *shinrin-yoku*) as a lifestyle is well known to the Japanese people. It has now become a recognized relaxation and stress management activity worldwide. Taiwan is positioned well to engage in forest bathing as part of its outdoor leisure activities because the country has 60% forest coverage and a strong connection with Japanese culture. Taiwan has begun scholarly exchange with Japanese authorities to initiate further collaborations. Overall, the total forest land in Taiwan is about 2.2 million ha, which provides ample space for its population. In fact, since 1965, the Taiwan Forestry Bureau has been establishing public recreation sites. Now, there are 18 national forest recreation areas, hundreds of nature trails, and dozens of forestry culture parks, forest railways, and forest parks. With significant awareness of health and mental health issues, the public turns to nature for an answer. Because forest bathing is easily accessible and relatively low risk, it has become a popular outdoor activity for all ages.

With the outbreak of the COVID-19 pandemic, people's lives have been changed, sometimes permanently. With proper social distancing, outdoor activities such as forest bathing can be managed and enjoyed. In Taiwan, visits to the outdoors, such as national parks, public beaches, marinas, dog parks, plazas, and public gardens, have increased by 17% since March 2020. It speaks to people's desire to be in touch with nature, and in Taiwan, outdoor activities such as hiking and nature forest bathing play an important role in their leisure needs as well as enhancing their physical and mental health.

Technological Advances Influence Research

Many technological instruments allow humans to better understand beneficial and adverse well-being effects of landscapes. Tools are used to collect environmental data (e.g. air quality, light, amount and type of vegetation) and to measure humans' physical changes in heart (PPG, ECG, HRV), blood (BP, SpO_2), saliva (cortisol, alpha amylase, DHEAS), brain (EEG) functions, and more.[1] Clinical measures, including those for autonomic nervous system effects and sensory metrics such as olfaction, tactile, and visual stimulation have become more sophisticated (Hansen *et al.*, 2017). Now common technology like cell phones and smart watches can be used in Global Positioning System (GPS) tracking and to measure blood pressure, heart rate variability, electroencephalography, accelerometry, and even respiration during sleep. A plethora of other measuring devices (e.g. the Emotiv, Muse, Polar chest straps, handheld sensors, stick-on sensors, special glasses/goggles, hat circuit boards) are available. Instrumentation common in medical practice used to measure changes both in the laboratory and *in situ* are becoming more available and portable, increasing research reach. Field measurements of clinical outcomes such as heart rate, hormone levels, oxygen saturation, and blood pressure have become more accurate over time. Many laboratory studies help find direction for field studies, and field studies help direct those in the laboratory.

New technology such as virtual reality (VR) and eye-tracking research can help pinpoint nuances. For example, Q. Huang *et al.* (2020) examined the effects of three types of urban VR environments—a courtyard with grass, a courtyard with trees, and a courtyard devoid of any vegetation—and confirmed greater positive affective reaction to natural VR environments than the concrete. A.S.H. Huang and Lin (2020) used eye tracking to better understand viewing behavior and the role of visual perception in people's landscape preferences. They found that higher hue variation and chroma encourage visual fixation;

higher visual fixation related positively to landscape preferences people had for the mountain, aquatic, and forest landscapes presented.

Likewise, advances in remote sensing allow more accurate and higher resolution measures of vegetation cover. Using high-density airborne laser scanning, an active remote-sensing technology that uses light detection and ranging imagery instruments to produce three-dimensional (3D) metrics on vegetation, Donovan *et al.* (2019) were able to discern that both increased vegetation height and variation in vegetation height were protective (homogeneous grass fields low in height were not) against small for gestational age (SGA) birth. SGA babies are smaller than most other babies of the same gestational age and are at risk of greater health problems during pregnancy, delivery, and after. Previous studies had only two-dimensional (2D) imagery available, which did not achieve this definition in vegetation description. These studies showed that increased height in vegetation was protective but missed the positive influence of heterogeneous landscapes. Areas with larger amounts of vegetation typically have better air quality, which offered a competing explanation. However, the use of more detailed 3D imaging helped researchers to reject this explanation because areas with more leaf surface were not necessarily the ones with the fewer SGAs. These results indicate that biodiversity may contribute to well-being in urban landscape designs.

Other explanations about the value of heterogeneous landscape types may include that they are aesthetically pleasing, reduce stress, and are psychologically restorative, or perhaps heterogeneous landscapes encourage people to spend more time outdoors, promoting social connectivity. Increased social connectivity is associated with improvements with a broad range of health outcomes (Rugel *et al.*, 2019), thus opening the door for more research. Additionally, some studies suggest that the strongest positive response to tree cover is for women with low levels of education (Hystad *et al.*, 2014; Dzhambov *et al.*, 2019; Laurent *et al.*, 2019).

Research Informs Practice and Practice Informs Research

Robust research strengthens our ability to make recommendations for practice. Within healthcare, research offers a path toward cost savings through fewer visits to the doctor for employees or prisoners as well as improved patient and staff satisfaction and improved medical outcomes, including moving sooner from intensive or acute care to less costly care units, lower infection occurrence, reduced pain and intake of costly analgesics, improved sleep, and reduced stress/anxiety for patients, family/visitors, and employees.

Van Esch *et al.*'s (2019) research applied to employee well-being exemplifies a potential cost-effective intervention of window views or images of pleasing outside environments. Once installed, this passive intervention requires no effort from employees and operates on a more-or-less continuous basis as compared with well-being interventions that require training, a designated time or place, or motivation to engage in an activity.

Well known to the outdoor recreation, leisure, and tourism fields, people often experience wonder, amazement, or reverence—summarized as awe—with regard to natural landscapes. This practice of taking people to places that inspire awe helped initiate awe research, which examines the healing effects of natural landscapes, among other outcomes (Zhang and Keltner, 2016). Research, in turn, helps practitioners identify and strengthen practices that may enhance awe (see Chapter 4, this volume).

It is morally and ethically responsible to connect research about well-being and natural landscapes to factors such as community revitalization, affordable housing, neighborhood walkability, food security, job creation, and youth engagement (Jennings *et al.*, 2017). In addition to potentially increasing the health and well-being for people, this sort of research can save healthcare dollars and specifically benefit disadvantaged people, who have been limited by structural racism and classism. Understanding the impact of demographics or familiarity on landscape preferences can help direct policy, historical area preservation, urban park development, and landscaping for buildings to be better tailored to community preferences, resulting in increased wellness benefits.

More studies will likely add new discoveries and nuances, resulting in practical evidence for landscape planners who can expand the restorative effects of urban environments and facilities. While more research is needed, the evidence is robust enough to act upon—pointing to practical implications ranging from policy decisions and urban landscape design to educational initiatives and new forms of therapy. In the following chapters we present some of these applications and design strategies.

Note

[1] BP, blood pressure; DHEAS, dehydroepiandrosterone sulfate; ECG, electrocardiogram; EEG, electroencephalogram; HRV, heart rate variability; PPG, photoplethysmography; SpO_2, oxygen saturation.

References

Antonelli, M., Donelli, D., Barbieri, G., Valussi, M., Maggini, V., *et al.* (2020) Forest volatile organic compounds and their effects on human health: a state-of-the-art review. *International Journal of Environmental Research and Public Health* 17(18): 6506.

Bach Pagès, A., Peñuelas, J., Clarà, J., Llusià, J., Campillo i López, F., *et al.* (2020) How should forests be characterized in regard to human health? Evidence from existing literature. *International Journal of Environmental Research and Public Health* 17(3): 1027.

Baxter, D.E. and Pelletier, L.G. (2019) Is nature relatedness a basic human psychological need? A critical examination of the extant literature. *Canadian Psychology/Psychologie Canadienne* 60(1): 21.

Berger, R. (2020) Nature therapy: incorporating nature into arts therapy. *Journal of Humanistic Psychology* 60(2), 244–257.

Browning, M.H.E.M., Saeidi-Rizi, F., McAnirlin, O., Yoon, H. and Pei, Y. (2020a) The role of methodological choices in the effects of experimental exposure to simulated natural landscapes on human health and cognitive performance: a systematic review. *Environment and Behavior* 23 February. https://doi.org/10.1177%2F0013916520906481

Browning, M.H., Shipley, N., McAnirlin, O., Becker, D., Yu, C.P., *et al.* (2020b) An actual natural setting improves mood better than its virtual counterpart: a meta-analysis of experimental data. *Frontiers in Psychology* 11: 2200.

Chiang, Y.C., Li, D. and Jane, H.A. (2017) Wild or tended nature? The effects of landscape location and vegetation density on physiological and psychological responses. *Landscape and Urban Planning* 167, 72–83.

Donovan, G.H., Gatziolis, D., Jakstis, K. and Comess, S.J.H.P. (2019) The natural environment and birth outcomes: comparting 3D exposure metrics derived from LiDAR to 2D metrics based on the normalized difference vegetation index. *Health & Place* 57, 305–312.

Dzhambov, A.M., Markevych, I. and Lercher, P. (2019) Associations of residential greenness, traffic noise, and air pollution with birth outcomes across Alpine areas. *Science of the Total Environment* 678, 399–408.

Franco, L.S., Shanahan, D.F. and Fuller, R.A. (2017) A review of the benefits of nature experiences: more than meets the eye. *International Journal of Environmental Research and Public Health* 14(8): 864.

Hansen, M.M. and Jones, R. (2020) The interrelationship of shinrin-yoku and spirituality: a scoping review. *The Journal of Alternative and Complementary Medicine* 26(12), 1093–1104.

Hansen, M.M., Jones, R. and Tocchini, K. (2017) Shinrin-yoku (forest bathing) and nature therapy: a state-of-the-art review. *International Journal of Environmental Research and Public Health* 14(8): 851.

Hidalgo, M.C., Berto, R., Galindo, M.P. and Getrevi, A. (2006) Identifying attractive and unattractive urban places: categories, restorativeness and aesthetic attributes. *Medio Ambiente y Comportamiento Humano* 7(2), 115–133.

Huang, A.S.H. and Lin, Y.J. (2020) The effect of landscape colour, complexity and preference on viewing behaviour. *Landscape Research* 45(2), 214–227.

Huang, Q., Yang, M., Jane, H.A., Li, S. and Bauer, N. (2020) Trees, grass, or concrete? The effects of different types of environments on stress reduction. *Landscape and Urban Planning* 193: 103654.

Hystad, P., Davies, H.W., Frank, L., Van Loon, J., Gehring, U., *et al.* (2014) Residential greenness and birth outcomes: evaluating the influence of spatially correlated built-environment factors. *Environmental Health Perspectives* 122(10), 1095–1102.

Ideno, Y., Hayashi, K., Abe, Y., Ueda, K., Iso, H., *et al.* (2017) Blood pressure-lowering effect of *Shinrin-yoku* (forest bathing): a systematic review and meta-analysis. *BMC Complementary and Alternative Medicine* 17(1): 409.

Jennings, V., Baptiste, A.K., Jelks, O. and Skeete, R. (2017) Urban green space and the pursuit of health equity in parts of the United States. *International Journal of Environmental Research and Public Health* 14(11): 1432.

Laurent, O., Benmarhnia, T., Milesi, C., Hu, J., Kleeman, M.J., *et al.* (2019) Relationships between greenness and low birth weight: investigating the interaction and mediation effects of air pollution. *Environmental Research* 175, 124–132.

Moeller, C., King, N., Burr, V., Gibbs, G.R. and Gomersall, T. (2018) Nature-based interventions in institutional and organisational settings: a scoping review. *International Journal of Environmental Health Research* 28(3), 293–305.

Montinari, M.R., Minelli, S. and De Caterina, R. (2019) The first 3500 years of aspirin history from its roots: a concise summary. *Vascular Pharmacology* 113, 1–8.

Naor, L. and Mayseless, O. (2020) The art of working with nature in nature-based therapies. *Journal of Experiential Education* 21 June. https://doi.org/10.1177%2F1053825920933639

Rosa, C.D., Larson, L.R., Collado, S., Cloutier, S. and Profice, C.C. (2020) Gender differences in connection to nature, outdoor preferences, and nature-based recreation among college students in Brazil and the United States. *Leisure Sciences* 1–21. https://doi.org/10.1080/01490 400.2020.1800538

Rugel, E.J., Carpiano, R.M., Henderson, S.B. and Brauer, M. (2019) Exposure to natural space, sense of community belonging, and adverse mental health outcomes across an urban region. *Environmental Research* 171, 365–377.

San Juan, C., Subiza-Pérez, M. and Vozmediano, L. (2017) Restoration and the city: the role of public urban squares. *Frontiers in Psychology* 8: 2093.

Satariano, B. and Gauci, R. (2019) Landform loss and its effect on health and well-being: the collapse of the Azure Window (Gozo) and the resultant reactions of the media and the Maltese community. In: Gauci, R. and Schembri, J.A. (eds) *Landscapes and Landforms of the Maltese Islands.* Springer, Cham, Switzerland, pp. 289–303.

Scopelliti, M., Carrus, G. and Bonaiuto, M. (2019) Is it really nature that restores people? A comparison with historical sites with high restorative potential. *Frontiers in Psychology* 9, 1–12.

Staats, H., Jahncke, H., Herzog, T.R. and Hartig, T. (2016) Urban options for psychological restoration: common strategies in everyday situations. *PLoS ONE* 11: e0146213.

Stigsdotter, U.K., Corazon, S.S., Sidenius, U., Kristiansen, J. and Grahn, P. (2017) It is not all bad for the grey city: a crossover study on physiological and psychological restoration in a forest and an urban environment. *Health & Place* 46, 145–154.

Subiza-Pérez, M., Vozmediano, L. and San Juan, C. (2019) Welcome to your plaza: assessing the restorative potential of urban squares through survey and objective evaluation methods. *Cities* 100: 102461.

Taylor, D.E. (2018) Racial and ethnic differences in connectedness to nature and landscape preferences among college students. *Environmental Justice* 11(3), 118–136.

Tilley, S., Neale, C., Patuano, A. and Cinderby, S. (2017) Older people's experiences of mobility and mood in an urban environment: a mixed methods approach using electroencephalography (EEG) and interviews. *International Journal of Environmental Research and Public Health* 14(2): 151.

Tsao, T.M., Tsai, M.J., Hwang, J.S., Cheng, W.F., Wu, C.F., *et al.* (2018) Health effects of a forest environment on natural killer cells in humans: an observational pilot study. *Oncotarget* 9(23), 16501–16511. https://doi.org/10.18632/oncotarget.24741

Ulrich, R.S. (1984) View through a window may influence recovery from surgery. *Science* 224(4647), 420–421.

van den Berg, A.E., Joye, Y. and Koole, S.L. (2016) Why viewing nature is more fascinating and restorative than viewing buildings: a closer look at perceived complexity. *Urban Forestry & Urban Greening* 20, 397–401.

van Esch, E., Minjock, R., Colarelli, S.M. and Hirsch, S. (2019) Office window views: view features trump nature in predicting employee well-being. *Journal of Environmental Psychology* 64, 56–64.

Velarde, M.D., Fry, G. and Tveit, M. (2007) Health effects of viewing landscapes: landscape types in environmental psychology. *Urban Forestry & Urban Greening* 6(4), 199–212.

Wang, R. and Zhao, J. (2017) Demographic groups' differences in visual preference for vegetated landscapes in urban green space. *Sustainable Cities and Society* 28, 350–357.

Zhang, J.W. and Keltner, D. (2016) Awe and the natural environment. *Encyclopedia of Mental Health* 1, 131–134.

6 Applications: Facilitating Healthy Connections with Nature

> The quality of life depends upon the ability of society to teach its members how to live in harmony with their environment—defined first as family, then with the community, then with the world and its resources.
>
> ~Ellen Swallow Richards (1842–1911), environmental chemist and founder of ecology

For most of the history of humankind, we have lived in close connection with natural landscapes. The industrial and post-industrial eras wrought large-scale changes in lifestyle, especially in the global North, leading to an estrangement from nature along with the rapid destabilization of the environment. Hope for the future lies with a growing group of global citizens, including Indigenous peoples, who increasingly recognize the need to act. Cultural historian and religious scholar Thomas Berry referred to this shift as the **Ecozoic era**—a time of transition in which we recover our relationship with the earth (Swimme and Berry, 1992). Other scholars and activists have referred to this shift in worldview as the **sustainability revolution**, the **ecological revolution**, and the **great turning**. Healthy connections to natural landscapes—and finding ways to facilitate this connection, utilizing both old and new (innovative) methods—is key to our collective well-being and survival.

Macy and Johnstone (2012) summarize three stories, or worldviews, that we tell about our connection to the earth; as humans, we have a choice as to which story we "buy into." **Business as usual** is the story told by the industrial growth society created by European-based colonial empires, which tells us to prioritize consumption to grow the economy. The second story, the **great unravelling**, draws attention to the many environmental and social disasters caused by the business-as-usual mindset, while the third story, the **great turning**, emphasizes an intentional shift toward a life-sustaining society. Having language and a vision for the kind of world we want to inhabit enables us to take concrete steps in that direction, including recognizing our role as a member of the biotic community. The COVID-19 pandemic, coupled with an intensified movement for racial justice revealing the racism and inequities faced by BIPOC (Black, Indigenous, People of Color) citizens of the USA and abroad, has exemplified both the great unravelling and the great turning. As the pandemic has forced many people to slow down, many have chosen to spend more time outdoors, renewing their recognition of the immense value of healthy relationships with natural landscapes and other people.

For millennia, natural landscapes have offered spaces of health, healing, and growth. While Western science may only be beginning (relatively speaking) to recognize and quantify these benefits, many cultural practices and philosophies are informed by connection to landscape, shaping norms over time. Some of these practices, such as horticultural therapy, are relatively modern and emphasize a specific approach related to particular settings or populations to facilitate healing. Others, such as herbalism, are very old (over 40,000 years, in fact) and are still effectively used in many cultures around the world (~75% of the world's population) and are now experiencing a re-emergence in dominant culture. Still others, such as **ecofeminism**, emerged at a specific point in time as a form of counterculture or resistance to dominant forces. These cultural practices may be used to help us negotiate the demands and challenges of today's world, particularly in terms of our relationship to landscape.

Applications

Access and connection to natural landscapes is largely influenced by the ways we prioritize our time, design our environments, and shape our societal institutions. While cultures in some "modern" societies, in places such as Scandinavia and Iceland, embrace nature as a way of life, it is common in most Westernized societies for nature to be pushed to the margins, if not explicitly feared and avoided (Mitten and Brymer, 2020). Developing healthy relationships to natural landscapes supports health and well-being, and having personal connections to places, including those under threat, encourages people to care for the environment and work for change. Research studies demonstrate promising practices for facilitating such healthy connections and are applicable to a variety of populations and settings. The extensive overlap in these different bodies of research show similar conclusions: exposure to natural landscapes is an essential part of human development, health, and healing.

Children

Nature is critical for healthy human development and is intertwined with human attachment from infancy.[1] Since the mid-20th century in the USA, experts from a number of fields have argued that children's experience of nature has exerted a crucial and irreplaceable effect on physical, cognitive, emotional, and spiritual development. However, a culture of fear that being outdoors exposes children to danger, highly structured schedules of education and activities, increased media consumption, and decreased access to natural landscapes have led to the dramatic reduction of outdoor play (Charles and Louv, 2020). Pyle (1993) and others have called this the "extinction of experience," which breeds apathy toward the very environment that we need for the survival of the human species (Soga and Gaston, 2016). The loss of children's contact with the natural world negatively impacts their development and sets the stage for continued environmental destruction. Young children develop emotional attachments to what is familiar and comfortable, so the more personal, positive, and appreciative their experiences with nature are, the more environmentally aware and active they will likely become (D'Amore and Chawla, 2020).

Research indicates that when children spend significant time immersed in natural landscapes, they experience benefits in cognitive flexibility, problem solving, creativity, self-esteem, self-discipline, higher standardized test scores, reduced effects of attention deficit disorder, and more (Charles and Louv, 2020). Positive direct experiences of nature, time outdoors with supportive adults, and membership/participation in environmental or nature-based organizations are the three most important factors related to environmental action in adulthood (D'Amore and Chawla, 2020). These factors implicate the importance of family outdoor experiences, as well as schools, camps, and other outdoor organizations.

Families

The amount of time spent in nature and children's views toward nature are greatly influenced by their families. In fact, the nature orientation of families has been found to be a stronger determinant of nature connection for Japanese children than levels of neighborhood urbanization (Soga *et al.*, 2018). Time spent in nature also facilitates family bonding and strengthens relationships between family members (Izenstark and Ebata, 2019; Overholt, 2019). Many families intentionally choose nature-based activities for health-promotion reasons and because they offer opportunity for ritual, escape from distractions of modern life, and bonding through shared experience (Izenstark and Ebata, 2016). Creating nature-based experiences for the whole family unit can facilitate these bonds and help parents introduce their children to nature, especially if the parents lack knowledge or comfort in the outdoors. One example of this is the family nature club. These organizations can positively impact household environmental behaviors, individual and family well-being, sense of community, social engagement, and amount of time spent in nature (D'Amore and Chawla, 2020). Since family time may be limited to weekends and vacations, nature connection through institutions such as schools and camps is also essential.

Schools, camps, and outdoor programs

Research shows that "greener" school settings promote health and academic success. For example, the relative amount of green space in school yards and surrounding environments may play a role in academic performance and overall well-being of students. Research studies have generally assessed factors such as tree cover and window views. For example, tree cover has been found to mitigate low mathematics scores in urban, high-poverty schools (Kuo *et al.*, 2018). But finding ways for children to engage with nature directly carries even greater benefit.

Forest kindergarten (often called *friluftsliv* in Scandinavia), a form of early childhood education that takes place primarily or entirely outdoors, is a cultural adaptation that ensures childhood connection to natural landscapes in the important formative years. These programs originated in Scandinavia and proliferated in Germany, where there are currently more than 1500 *waldkindergartens* in operation (Gregory, 2017). Children enrolled in these programs learn, grow, and explore in the natural environment, rain or shine. These programs are becoming increasingly popular worldwide, especially in Europe and North America, with the number of US schools nearly doubling between 2016 and 2017 (North American Association for Environmental Education (NAAEE), 2017). These educational settings rose in prominence in the COVID-19 era, as it became evident that being outdoors was a reliable way to reduce disease transmission.

Children and adults may also experience healthy nature connection through outdoor education (OE) venues such as camps, environmental education (EE), and adventure education (AE) programming. Camps range in format from themed day camps to overnight camps, last anywhere from several days to the entire summer season, and take place mostly out of doors, providing children with an immersive nature experience. Research on camps shows an ability to assist in the developmental process, impacting social skills, leadership, environmental awareness, self-esteem, independence, adventure and exploration, friendship skills, decision making, values, and spirituality (Garst *et al.*, 2011; Richmond *et al.*, 2019). The American Camp Association reported in 2017 that over 14,000 camps exist in the USA, attended by over 14 million children and adults each year.

AE is a branch of OE primarily concerned with interpersonal and intrapersonal relationships, which are developed through adventurous activities, often requiring problem solving, communication, and personal challenge (Priest and Gass, 2017). Documented benefits associated with AE are numerous, including: (i) leadership development;

(ii) empowerment; (iii) self-efficacy; (iv) confidence; (v) positive self-concept; (vi) psychological resilience; and (vii) knowledge of environmental issues (Sibthorp *et al.*, 2007). EE programs represent another branch of OE concerned with ecosystem relationships, including humans' role as ecosystem members. Key tenets of EE include environmental literacy and integrity, social equity, and shared prosperity to create a sustainable future for all (NAAEE, 2017). It is easy to assume that the immersive nature experiences of AE and EE programming will automatically lead people to deepen their relationship with nature, but this may not always be the case—someone may instead develop an adversarial relationship (e.g. "conquering" the mountain) or be so overwhelmed by environmental problems that they shut down. To avoid these types of outcomes, educators should work to deliberately nurture a sense of place and connection to landscape, using techniques such as place-responsive pedagogy (Mannion *et al.*, 2013).

For example, citizen science represents one such practice. By enlisting members of the public to make and record useful observations, such as tracking wildflower blooms or counting aquatic invertebrates, volunteers can collect valuable research data. In return, such projects increase participants' connections to science, place, and nature, while supporting science literacy and environmental stewardship (Dickinson *et al.*, 2012). Citizen science may help to reverse the reduction of experience that results from declining opportunities for exposure to nature and that contributes to decreasing conservation attitudes (Schuttler *et al.*, 2018). Volunteers are engaged in community development while learning about nature, developing a sense of place/place attachment and providing a service, which helps develop an ethic of care.

Another means of developing a healthy relationship to place is through the practice of mindfulness. Recent studies show links between mindful practices and connection to nature, strengthening place-based education, facilitating spiritual connections, and cultivating feelings of interrelatedness (Deringer, 2017; Adams and Beauchamp, 2020). This relationship is bidirectional; that is, mindfulness can enhance connectedness to nature, and connection to nature can promote mindfulness (Nisbet *et al.*, 2019).

Therapeutic applications

A variety of therapeutic modalities that rely on exposure to natural landscapes or to some element of nature have (re)emerged, primarily in Westernized countries and often in response to the failure of allopathic medicine to produce satisfactory results. These applications, presented in Table 6.1, represent movement toward a more holistic view of the connection between humans and nature, yet they still reside within the dominant worldview (and therefore remain separate practices despite their obvious similarities).

Table 6.1 captures a small sample of existing practices. Readers are encouraged to use this as a starting point to learn more. There is a global movement to recognize nature as a public health intervention strategy. Each of these therapeutic applications fits within this vision, as do other practices described throughout this book. To achieve this vision, there is still work to be done to make nature accessible to all, especially low income and people of color.

Table 6.1. Therapeutic applications.

Research area	Synopsis of findings[a]
Animals	Connection to animals can facilitate health through sustenance/medicine, companionship, spirituality, teaching, and certain forms of therapy. For example, animal–human relationships are important in the promotion of health and cultural cohesion in Indigenous communities (McGinnis *et al.*, 2019). Animal-assisted therapy has demonstrated effectiveness with autism spectrum disorders, medical issues, behavioral challenges, and emotional well-being (Nimer and Lundahl, 2007; Bystrom *et al.*, 2019).
Ecopsychology/ ecotherapy	**Ecopsychology** blends environmental philosophy, ecology, and psychology to explore the connection between our psychological health and the ecological health of the earth. The term "ecopsychology" was coined in 1963 by Robert Greenway (1999) and in its early conceptions was informed by ecofeminism. Ecopsychology specifically focuses on the interconnectedness of our psyches and the natural world, and the ways our alienation has resulted in destructive behavior toward the environment, spotlighting the environmental crisis as a psychological crisis. Some people call the actual applied practice of ecopsychology **ecotherapy** or **nature therapy**, while others look at these as three names for the same practice.
Horticultural therapy	Horticultural therapy (HT) has been recognized as a professional field in the USA since at least the 1920s as a subset of occupational therapy. Today, HT is described as "participation in horticultural activities facilitated by a registered horticultural therapist to achieve specific goals within an established treatment, rehabilitation, or vocational plan" (American Horticultural Therapy Association, n.d.). HT has been utilized with people who have physical, mental, psychological, or developmental disabilities, victims of abuse, prisoners, veterans, young children, and older adults, especially those residing in care facilities or suffering from dementia (e.g. Wong *et al.*, 2020).
Nature prescriptions	US physicians have prescribed time in natural settings since at least the 1800s when urban families escaped polluted city environments by visiting sanatoriums, seashores, and the mountains of the west (Crnic and Kondo, 2019). Over time, modern medicine became more reliant on technology and distanced itself from environmentally-based practices. However, this trend has recently re-emerged, with the recognition of the benefits of landscapes for lifestyle-related diseases. Park or nature prescriptions are gaining momentum as a way for trusted authority figures (healthcare providers) to encourage children and families to access nearby nature spaces for physical activity and health. Robert Zarr, founder of Park Rx America, has said nature prescriptions have four essential features—place, dose, activity, and frequency—and they provide an important link between the body of evidence and the practice of spending time outdoors (Zarr *et al.*, 2020). Preliminary data show increases in park use for families receiving a park prescription, and physicians report an increased awareness of the benefits of talking about spending time in nature with their patients (Razani *et al.*, 2020). Issues exist regarding funding, access, and ability for families to "fill" these prescriptions, but as this practice gains momentum, solutions arise. For example, insurance companies are beginning to provide incentives for park prescriptions, and financial assistance/cooperation is increasing from the outdoor industry and land management agencies (Rueben, 2019).

Continued

Table 6.1. Continued.

Research area	Synopsis of findings[a]
Veteran programming	Adventure and nature-based experiences can assist veterans in transitioning back to civilian life and managing symptoms related to post-traumatic stress, traumatic brain injury, depression, and other mental and physical health issues. Many of these programs involve short-term (4–7 days), group-based nature experiences, such as an Outward Bound course (Ewert, 2014) or a fly-fishing program (Bennett *et al.*, 2017). These studies show positive outcomes for veterans on a range of measures (Duvall and Kaplan, 2014) and may be applicable to other populations coping with similar issues.
Virtual nature/ technology	While access to "real" nature is preferable, there are certain situations, such as incarceration, mobility constraints, or medical procedures, where spending time outdoors may be undesirable or impossible (White *et al.*, 2018). Virtual nature experiences may provide another way to receive some of the benefits of connecting to natural landscapes, with the requisite technology being increasingly accessible and affordable (Tanja-Dijkstra *et al.*, 2018). This body of research considers the therapeutic effects of virtual nature for pain relief, anxiety reduction, rehabilitation, distraction/relaxation during medical treatments, and treatment of mental health issues (White *et al.*, 2018).
Wilderness therapy	Wilderness therapy, also called outdoor behavioral healthcare and in Australia bush adventure therapy (BAT), is a modality that utilizes immersive nature experiences and adventure activities as a setting for intensive therapeutic work. Many of these programs are geared toward adolescents with behavioral, mental health, or substance abuse issues, and a growing body of research documents its efficacy (Harper and Dobud, 2021). Critics of wilderness therapy point to the high costs of such programs (both time and monetary) as well as to issues of consent and unethical practices in a small minority of programs. Recent studies have measured treatment outcomes to further legitimize the modality and work toward medical insurance coverage (Gillis *et al.*, 2016). For example, Gass *et al.* (2019) found that wilderness therapy is significantly more effective than office therapy for adolescents.

[a]Bold text indicates a new term.

Diversity

A common narrative exists, especially in the USA, that suggests that BIPOC people do not participate in outdoor recreation. This narrative, often supported by statistics such as visitation rates to national parks, shows that despite making up about 14% of the US population, African Americans make up between 4% and 6% of national park visitors. Statistics such as this are commonly "explained" by well-meaning people who think that lack of park visitation stems from surface-level issues such as lack of money, interest, or skill level. While this may be true (and is also true for some people of all races), it ignores the underlying history of racism and exclusion in the history of the USA, including the environmental movement (Finney, 2014).

The stereotype that Black people are uninterested in parks stems from White supremacy embedded in the park system, especially in US southern states, where this untruth has supported unequal facilities and discrimination (O'Brien, 2015). The outdoor/environmental community must address the fact that most lands currently utilized for outdoor pursuits are stolen lands that once belonged to Indigenous peoples, and that the enduring legacy of racism and slavery in the USA has created generational trauma, sometimes related to the land/landscape itself. The effects of slavery and the Jim Crow era has led many African Americans to both avoid outdoor spaces out of safety concerns and create spaces of their own, including state parks and beaches (Finney, 2014). While many of these parks no longer exist due to discriminatory practices relative to loss of funding, several important beaches remain, thanks in large part to tireless advocacy from Black environmentalists such as MaVynee Betsch for American Beach on Amelia Island, Florida.

There is an important legacy of BIPOC outdoor leaders, athletes, and environmentalists who have made great contributions to their fields, despite the very real racism and discrimination they faced. The emergence of more clubs and groups with BIPOC leadership and membership, such as Backyard Basecamp in Baltimore or the Greening Youth Foundation in Atlanta, is one strategy to help individuals to feel safe and connected to community while experiencing the benefits of healthy relationships with natural landscapes. These groups provide important mentorship to young people, potentially helping them see outdoor careers and pursuits as an option for themselves.

Finally, dominant culture has a tendency to ignore or dismiss the wealth of ancient environmental knowledge/experience contained in BIPOC communities related to medicine, ecology, agriculture, sustenance, navigation, and more. When accessed with respect and compassion, this cultural knowledge can inform our choices about interacting with natural landscapes in the future.

Outdoor or nature-based therapy at the Ramon Crater in the Negev desert, Israel. Photo by Lia Naor, PhD, nature therapist and researcher.

Israel: Nature-based interventions in a rich and diverse landscape
By Lia Naor

Israel is a small country (13,714 km²), with a multicultural population of a little under 9 million. The population of Israel is diverse, encompassing a variety of cultures, religions, and geographic backgrounds from around the world, contributing to a unique social and cultural mosaic. Israel is situated between Africa, Asia, and Europe and features a rich and diverse ecosystem and unique geography consisting of snowcapped mountains in the north, a long coastal plain in the west, and a large desert from the center to the south of the country bordering with the Red Sea. The majority of the population in Israel has developed a personal connection with the landscape, whether through youth group activities, army service, or agriculture. The rich historical and geographical connection people have with the land has resulted in the development of various nature-based interventions in educational and therapeutic frameworks in Israel.

Nature-based therapies have developed in Israel to provide clinical populations with experiential and physical therapeutic alternatives to traditional interventions when these do not suffice. Civilians live in a country where their existence is constantly threatened by war with many required to serve in the military, so the population of Israel is relatively experienced in outdoor conduct and survival skills. These civilians, as well as veterans, are confronted with life-threatening situations, and many suffer from physical disabilities and post-trauma as a result of this situation. I believe that the existential and historical roots of the Israeli society have greatly influenced the development of nature-based interventions in Israel, as well as the way these are implemented. From this perspective, nature-based interventions that involve connections to the land, and wilderness and adventure therapy that focus on challenging outdoor skills and competencies, are developed by professionals with expertise in outdoor interventions and group facilitation and are acknowledged as accepted and beneficial modes of intervention in Israel.

Being such a small country with limited areas of wilderness has led the majority of outdoor programmers to carry out their therapeutic interventions in the south of Israel, which is desert land encompassing the Judaean Desert and Negev Desert. The Judaean Desert is situated between Jerusalem and the Dead Sea and is the smallest desert in the world. In fact, it is north of the geographical global desert line and was created by clouds showering rain on the mountains of Jerusalem and drifting east, leaving a small but unique desert going from high mountain ranges down to the lowest place on earth, characterized by deep riverbeds and high waterfalls. But the significance of this desert lies not only in the geological and botanical diversity but in a land rich of hermits, saints, spiritual sects, and leaders who have found inner peace and significant insights in the solace of the desert.

The Negev Desert is vast, providing us with a variety of areas to journey through in wilderness programs. The significance of journeying through desert land in Israel may be linked to the history of the Jewish people who walked through the desert for 40 years on their way to the land of Israel. In this period, the generation of Israelites who were slaves in Egypt died, and a new generation was born. In this time, the Bible was given, and the people became a community based on mutual values. These ancient stories are a very strong metaphor for wilderness therapy in Israel, embedding the possibility of a symbolic death and rebirth toward personal and communal transformation, which is the therapeutic objective for many of us in our work.

Other Cultural Frameworks

Many of the perspectives presented in this chapter emerged from the cultural context of Western science. Considering other models and ways of understanding our relationship with natural landscapes may aid us in choosing a path forward that honors our individual connections to landscapes and harbors intellectual diversity and global solutions. Macy and Johnstone (2012) argued that we need a cultural shift, and that if we step back and look, we may see that it is already underway; they wrote, "We live at a time when a new view of reality is emerging, where spiritual insight and scientific discovery both contribute to our understanding of ourselves as intimately interwoven with our world" (p. 32).

Traditional ecological knowledge

Sometimes referred to as Indigenous knowledge or native science, traditional ecological knowledge (TEK) generally refers to knowledge, practices, and beliefs about the natural world held by Indigenous peoples and influenced by culture, worldview, and bioregion (Whyte, 2013).[2] TEK has also been conceptualized as a set of responsibilities and construed in terms of relationships with and respect for the non-human world. In other words, TEK is not just a body of knowledge; it is a way of being. Just as there is not only one Indigenous culture or society, there is no single interpretation or definition of TEK. Whyte suggested that TEK is most usefully seen as a collaborative concept that invites different populations to learn from one another, beginning with an interrogation of what "knowledge" is and then considering its application across various forms of environmental governance (e.g. native reservations, state and federal parks, forests, etc.). This diversity of thought can help us all learn to better steward lands and respond to pressing issues of climate change.

An important feature of TEK is that it recognizes that adaptation to our natural environment is key to human survival and uses observation and practices spanning generations to understand the natural environment's response to human activities. Indigenous groups practicing TEK in their area offer perspectives, insights, and knowledge that can be different or complementary to what present-day ecologists and land managers understand. Using TEK to enhance ecosystem resilience is an area especially useful to conservation professionals. However, Western scientists have a long history of denial of the existence and validity of Indigenous knowledge and too often want to use TEK to increase their control over the environment without valuing or including the inherent spiritual foundations and Indigenous values and worldviews (Simpson, 2004). This leads to further marginalization of Indigenous people. To truly understand TEK, respect and regard must be given to the originating cultures.

Kimmerer (2002) suggests that TEK and scientific ecological knowledge (SEK) are parallel and complementary traditions. While both traditions hold an empirical body of knowledge regarding ecological relationships, TEK also "offers an alternative to the dominant consumptive values of Western societies" (Kimmerer, 2002, p. 434). This is because, unlike Western science that purports to be value free, TEK affirms being inseparable from social and spiritual aspects of its culture and "includes an ethic of reciprocal respect and obligation between humans and the nonhuman world" (Kimmerer, 2002, p. 434). She suggests that incorporating TEK into science curriculums allows for a multicultural perspective that not only deepens cross-cultural relationships but encourages students and teachers to begin to understand the cultural assumptions underlying Western traditions as well. Awakening personal and spiritual connections to the non-human natural world while deepening ecological understanding may help deepen our relationships to all nature, including one another. One way of doing this is through the practice of pilgrimages.

Pilgrimages and iconic landforms

Walking pilgrimages, combining physical activity with personal and spiritual encounters in natural landscapes, have a distinct role in human–landscape interactions. Often thought of as special or sacred journeys, these phenomena are simultaneously site specific, social, and individual. Humans have engaged in pilgrimages—secular and non-secular—likely longer than recorded history. Pilgrimages include famous trails like the El Camino de Santiago in Spain, as well as quiet journeys to places special to a single family. Some pilgrimages' landscapes are connected to actions in history such as Salt Satyagraha that honors the 1930 non-violent 24-day protest march led by Mahatma Gandhi. Most pilgrimages are connected to sacred sites, one such pilgrimage being the Kumbh Mela in India at the confluence of the rivers Ganges, Yamuna, and Saraswati. During the 55-day religious occasion, millions of people pilgrimage to the site for restorative and sin-cleansing dips or communal washing in the waters. For context, 150 million people participated in 2019, whereas the world's largest city has 37 million people.

Pilgrimages are often therapeutic, leading to better health and well-being. Warfield's (2018) research using accounts of pilgrims' experiences and photographs demonstrated how journeys on the North Wales Pilgrim's Way enabled participants to forge connections with the natural environment and local heritage, as well as the emotional–spiritual aspects of their lives. They reported improved biological health (e.g. lower blood pressure and an increase in physical health because of the training and the time on the journey) and increases in psychological well-being (e.g. connections with others that can continue after the pilgrimage; a sense of belonging and identity; a spiritual sense of connectedness to others and a higher power).

Many people seek physical, psychological, and spiritual respite in the natural world through vacations and other intentional journeys, such as pilgrimages; therefore, countries such as Japan, Norway, and Sweden are incorporating pilgrimage routes and infrastructure into their economic growth plans. Rapid growth in pilgrimage journeys and other nature-based travel call for a focus on sustainability and a conscious effort to build stronger bridges between conservation groups, pilgrimage communities, and local communities.

Many sacred places and pilgrimages are associated with ancient cultures and Indigenous people, though non-Indigenous people often are the recent researchers. For example, the Mateo Tepee or Grizzly Bear Lodge has long been a vision quest site for a number of American Indian tribes. Named Devils Tower by White surveyors in Wyoming in 1875, and designated the first US national monument in 1906, over 20,000 climbing ascents have been made on this sacred site. Indigenous voices—too often disregarded—should be included in joint management strategies for social tourism, ecotourism, and pilgrimages, all blooming efforts globally with their popularity likely to be fueled by 2020 pandemic considerations.

Aimed at benefiting local societies, research about the effects of social tourism (a kind of community-based tourism) demonstrates it can engender respect for Indigenous traditions and contribute to the economic well-being of these communities. Pyke *et al.* (2019) examined the effects of a 1-day social tourism event on low-income families from a First Nation community in Alaska. Their results showed improved subjective well-being in family relations, social life, material well-being, and leisure, and that these effects were shaped by gender and age. For the Nharo Bushmen in Botswana, Apelian (2013) proposed restorative ecotourism, social tourism focused specifically on sustaining Indigenous culture, with the Nharo heading the joint management. As Apelian said, they "hold true connection—to self, each other, and the land around them" (p. 13), which offers tourists education about their wisdom, spirituality, and worldview. These results have significant practical implications for education, conservation, and policy-related development, especially when consistent care is taken to avoid Indigenous cultural displays contrived through a Western gaze.

Friluftsliv

Another example of culturally informed connection to the natural world is evidenced in early 19th-century Norwegian culture. When Henrik Ibsen presented *friluftsliv* over 150 years ago, it was mystical and captured the hearts of the Norwegian populace. Roughly translated, the word means "free air life" and now describes a philosophical lifestyle or a way of life, embedded in Norwegian and general Scandinavian culture. It is characterized by a sense of freedom in nature and a spiritual connectedness with the landscape (Gelter, 2000).

At the beginning of the 18th century, Norway had been struggling for freedom from Denmark and Sweden for almost 500 years. A creative middle class decided to give becoming a free nation a try. They shunned Bacon's slogan for the paradigm of modernity, "Knowledge is power over nature," deciding instead to use the Swiss philosopher Jean-Jacques Rousseau's terminology "noble savages" for the inhabitants of the European alpine lake regions (Faarlund *et al.*, 2007). The philosophy originated as part of a protest movement of European artists and philosophers against the reductionist, natural science mentality of the early 19th century. By the 20th century, Norway had done what no other European nation had been able to do; by identifying with nature and the concept of *friluftsliv*, it achieved freedom without militant nationalism.

Friluftsliv became a cultural tradition with health benefits and has evolved into understanding that free nature has intrinsic value. In the 1970s, *friluftsliv* developed as an academic field, heavily influenced by the deep ecology movement. It is currently taught in a variety of ways, including in early childhood through *friluftsliv* kindergartens, as a year of study for students prior to entering the workforce or college, and as a college major. In this way, *friluftsliv* is passed on to future generations and is well established as part of Norwegian culture.

Akin to the romantic movement in the USA, inspiration for *friluftsliv* philosophy was rooted in nature–culture dualism inherent to romanticism and has been criticized for being egalitarian and emphasizing men and masculinity in the outdoors (Gurholt, 2008). However, humans are creators of culture and therefore able to respond to previous practices and ideas to create new culture. In this vein, Gurholt (2014) demonstrated that *friluftsliv* has grown and changed along with Norwegian culture over time and proposed a cultural–ecological approach, emphasizing embodied experience of the natural world as a way to understand the transformative potential of nature experiences. The concept of *friluftsliv* provides identity as well as the opportunity to be in nature receiving many health benefits.

Conclusion

To rekindle a healthy relationship with the earth, especially in Westernized cultures, we must first recognize that humans are part of the natural environment—not separate or above it. Through this recognition, we may be able to divert our energy from the dominant ideals of individualism, consumerism, and domination over nature, and instead embrace systems thinking and focus on community and environmental sustainability. We must conclude that natural landscapes are not something to be *used* to aid our health, but rather to be in relationship with—and by doing so, we benefit the health of all beings.

Ecofeminism is a philosophy and area of study that offers wisdom and guidance in this approach; a synthesis of feminist socialism and ecology, it represents the understanding that the health of earth and survival of humans is tightly bound with economics, reproductive rights, and women's liberation. It recognizes and works to change the subordination of nature, poor people, children, Indigenous people, and women.

Francoise d'Eaubonne (1974), a feminist activist, coined the term ecofeminism on the premise that society's disregard for women was comparable to its degradation of nature. She understood how impacts on the biosphere, questions of energy choices, genetic engineering, and women's reproductive rights were concrete manifestations of the intersections of feminism and ecology. Critics of ecofeminism have dismissed it as unnecessary, anti-men, elitist, angry, or irrelevant/dismissive to women of color and poor people. In recent years, however, ecofeminist work has become more explicitly intersectional, recognizing that the freedom of humanity is dependent on the freedom of all people, and that one's relationship with the natural environment does not solely depend on any one characteristic such as race or gender but rather a combination of factors (Kings, 2017). Expressing these associations, Collins (1974) wrote, "Racism, sexism, class exploitation, and ecological destruction are four interlocking pillars upon which the structure of the patriarchy rests" (p. 161). Through ecofeminism, the interconnectedness of all types of domination can be seen and begun to be dismantled. It offers and asks for a critique of culture and nature and identifies dualism as an ideology and mechanism used to degrade the "other."

Climate change and issues of overconsumption cannot be solved solely by the "masculinist techno-science approaches" that created them, but rather need the tactics and ideologies of ecofeminism that have been utilized worldwide to focus on relationships between global economic policies and global ecological crises (Gaard, 2015). As exemplified by the work of Indian scholar and environmental activist Vandana Shiva (2016), the goal of ecofeminism is to increase the joint health and welfare of humans and nature.

As individuals, we can choose to inhabit the story of the great turning by engaging in three kinds of acts, or what Macy and Johnstone (2012) called **dimensions**: (i) holding actions; (ii) life-sustaining systems and practices; and (iii) shifts in consciousness. Holding actions are the choices that we make politically, economically, and socially—for example protests or boycotts—to slow the destruction of the natural environment. Life-sustaining systems and practices involve rethinking the way we do things, such as creating community gardens or engaging in nature-based therapies. Finally, shifts in consciousness involve deepening our connection to the earth and to each other as we recreate and reinforce the values we want our societies to hold. Cultural practices and philosophies, such as ecofeminism and TEK, describe different ways of doing this. Little by little, we can choose healthy relationships over growth and work toward a world that values all living things. In the next chapter, we present ideas of structuring physical space as movement toward this goal.

Notes

[1] For in-depth treatment on child development and nature, please see Ewert *et al.* (2014), Chapter 5.

[2] Traditional ecological knowledge (TEK) and traditional Indigenous knowledge (TIK) (referred to in Chapter 4, this volume) are different. TEK is knowledge about the natural world and how to work with it, whereas TIK is all of the knowledge of Indigenous people as well as about who has the knowledge (Indigenous people). For further treatment on TEK, please see Ewert *et al.* (2014), Chapter 6.

References

Adams, D. and Beauchamp, G. (2020) A study of the experiences of children aged 7–11 taking part in mindful approaches in local nature reserves. *Journal of Adventure Education and Outdoor Learning* 4 March, 1–10. https://doi.org/10.1080/14729679.2020.1736110

American Horticultural Therapy Association (n.d.) Definitions and Positions Paper. Available at: https://www.ahta.org/assets/docs/definitions%20and%20positions%20final%206.17.pdf (accessed 31 January 2021).

Apelian, N.M. (2013) *Restorative Ecotourism as a Solution to Intergenerational Knowledge Retention: an Exploratory Study with Two Communities of San Bushmen in Botswana.* Prescott College, Prescott, Arizona.

Bennett, J., Piatt, J. and Van Puymbroeck, M. (2017) Outcomes of a therapeutic fly-fishing program for veterans with combat-related disabilities: a community-based rehabilitation initiative. *Community Mental Health Journal* 53(7), 756–765.

Bystrom, K., Grahn, P. and Hägerhäll, C. (2019) Vitality from experiences in nature and contact with animals: a way to develop joint attention and social engagement in children with autism? *International Journal of Environmental Research and Public Health* 16(23): 4673.

Charles, C. and Louv, R. (2020) Wild hope: the transformative power of children engaging with nature. In: Cutter-Mckenzie-Knowles, A., Malone, K. and Barrat Hacking, E. (eds) *Research Handbook on Childhoodnature: Assemblages of Childhood and Nature Research.* Springer, Cham, Switzerland, pp. 395–415.

Collins, S. (1974) *A Different Heaven and Earth.* Judson Press, Valley Forge, Pennsylvania.

Crnic, M. and Kondo, M.C. (2019) Nature Rx: reemergence of pediatric nature-based therapeutic programs from the late 19th and early 20th centuries. *American Journal of Public Health* 109(10), 1371–1378.

D'Amore, C. and Chawla, L. (2020) Significant life experiences that connect children with nature: a research review and applications to a family nature club. In: Cutter-Mckenzie-Knowles, A., Malone, K. and Barrat Hacking, E. (eds) *Research Handbook on Childhoodnature: Assemblages of Childhood and Nature Research.* Springer, Cham, Switzerland, pp. 799–825.

d'Eaubonne, F. (1974) Feminism or death. In: Marks, E. and de Courtivron, I. (eds) *New French Feminisms: an Anthology.* Schocken Books, New York, pp. 64–67.

Deringer, S.A. (2017) Mindful place-based education: mapping the literature. *Journal of Experiential Education* 404(4), 333–348.

Dickinson, J., Shirk, J., Bonter, D., Bonney, R., Crain, R.L., *et al.* (2012) The current state of citizen science as a tool for ecological research and public engagement. *Frontiers in Ecology and the Environment* 10(6), 291–297. doi: 10.1890/110236.

Duvall, J. and Kaplan, R. (2014) Enhancing the well-being of veterans using extended group-based nature recreation experiences. *Journal of Rehabilitation Research and Development* 51(5), 685–696.

Ewert, A. (2014) Military veterans and the use of adventure education experiences in natural environments for therapeutic outcomes. *Ecopsychology* 6(3), 155–164.

Ewert, A.W., Mitten, D.S. and Overholt, J.R. (2014) *Natural Environments and Human Health.* CAB International, Boston, Massachusetts.

Faarlund, N., Dahle, B. and Jensen, A. (2007) Nature is the home of culture – *friluftsliv* is a way home. In: Watson, A., Sproull, J. and Dean, L. (eds) *Science and Stewardship to Protect and Sustain Wilderness Values: Eighth World Wilderness Congress symposium:* September 30–October 6 2005, Anchorage, Alaska. USDA Forest Service Proceedings RMRS-P-49. United States Department of Agriculture (USDA), Forest Service, Rocky Mountain Research Station, Fort Collins, Colorado, 393–396.

Finney, C. (2014) *Black Faces White Spaces: Reimagining the Relationship of African Americans to the Great Outdoors.* The University of North Carolina Press, Chapel Hill, North Carolina.

Gaard, G. (2015) Ecofeminism and climate change. *Women's Studies International Forum* 49, 20–33.

Garst, B., Browne, L. and Bialeschki, M. (2011) Youth development and the camp experience. *New Directions for Youth Development* 2011(130), 73–87.

Gass, M.A., Wilson, T., Talbot, B., Tucker, A., Ugianskis, M., *et al.* (2019) The value of outdoor behavioral healthcare for adolescent substance users with comorbid conditions. *Substance Abuse: Research and Treatment* 13, 1–8.

Gelter, H. (2000) Friluftsliv: the Scandinavian philosophy of outdoor life. *Canadian Journal of Environmental Education (CJEE)* 5(1), 77–92.

Gillis, H.L., Speelman, E., Linville, N., Bailey, E., Kalle, A., *et al.* (2016) Meta-analysis of treatment outcomes measured by the Y-OQ and Y-OQ-SR comparing wilderness and non-wilderness treatment programs. *Child Youth Care Forum* 45, 851–863.

Greenway, R. (1999) Ecopsychology: a personal history. *Gatherings: Journal of the International Community for Ecopsychology* 1(1).

Gregory, A. (2017) Running free in Germany's outdoor preschools. *The New York Times Style Magazine* 18 May. Available at: https://www.nytimes.com/2017/05/18/t-magazine/germany-forest-kindergarten-outdoor-preschool-waldkitas.html (accessed 23 December 2020).

Gurholt, K.P. (2008) Norwegian *friluftsliv* and ideals of becoming an 'educated man'. *Journal of Adventure Education and Outdoor Learning* 8(1), 55–70.

Gurholt, K.P. (2014) Joy of nature, *friluftsliv* education and self: combining narrative and cultural: ecological approaches to environmental sustainability. *Journal of Adventure Education and Outdoor Learning* 14(3), 233–246.

Harper, N.J. and Dobud, W.W. (eds) (2021) *Outdoor Therapies: an Introduction to Practices, Possibilities, and Critical Perspectives.* Routledge, New York.

Izenstark, D. and Ebata, A. (2016) Theorizing family-based nature activities and family functioning: the integration of attention restoration theory with a family routines and rituals perspective. *Journal of Family Theory & Review* 8(2), 137–153.

Izenstark, D. and Ebata, A.T. (2019) Why families go outside: an exploration of mothers' and daughters' family-based nature activities. *Leisure Sciences* 1–19. https://doi.org/10.1080/01490400.2019.1625293

Kimmerer, R.W. (2002) Weaving traditional ecological knowledge into biological education: a call to action. *BioScience* 52(5), 432–438.

Kings, A. (2017) Intersectionality and the changing face of ecofeminism. *Ethics and the Environment* 22(1), 63–87.

Kuo, M., Browning, M., Sachdeva, S., Lee, K. and Westphal, L. (2018) Might school performance grow on trees? Examining the link between "greenness" and academic achievement in urban, high-poverty schools. *Frontiers in Psychology* 9. http://dx.doi.org//10.3389/fpsyg.2018.01669

Macy, J. and Johnstone, C. (2012) *Active Hope: How to Face the Mess We're in Without Going Crazy*. New World Library, Novato, California.

Mannion, G., Fenwick, A. and Lynch, J. (2013) Place-responsive pedagogy: learning from teachers' experiences of excursions in nature. *Environmental Education Research* 19(6), 792–809.

McGinnis, A., Kincaid, A., Barrett, M., Ham, C. and Community Elders Research Advisory Group (2019) Strengthening animal–human relationships as a doorway to Indigenous holistic wellness. *Ecopsychology* 11(3), 162–173.

Mitten, D. and Brymer, E. (2020) Outdoor and environmental education: nature and wellbeing. In: Peters, M. (ed.) *Encyclopedia of Teacher Education*. Springer, Singapore, p. 10. https://doi.org/10.1007/978-981-13-1179-6_365-1

Nimer, J. and Lundahl, B. (2007) Animal-assisted therapy: a meta-analysis. *Anthrozoös* 20(3), 225–238.

Nisbet, E., Zelenski, J. and Grandpierre, Z. (2019) Mindfulness in nature enhances connectedness and mood. *Ecopsychology* 11(2), 81–91.

North American Association for Environmental Education (NAAEE) (2017) *Nature Preschools and Forest Kindergartens: 2017 National Survey*. NAAEE, Washington, DC.

O'Brien, W. (2015) *Landscapes of Exclusion: State Parks and Jim Crow in the American South*. University of Massachusetts Press, Amherst, Massachusetts.

Overholt, J. (2019) Role shifts and equalizing experiences through father–child outdoor adventure programs. *Leisure Sciences* 1–20. https://doi.org/10.1080/01490400.2019.1627966

Priest, S. and Gass, M. (2017) *Effective Leadership in Adventure Programming, 3E*. Human Kinetics, Champaign, Illinois.

Pyke, J., Pyke, S. and Watuwa, R. (2019) Social tourism and well-being in a first nation community. *Annals of Tourism Research* 77, 38–48.

Pyle, R.M (1993) *The Thunder Tree: Lessons from an Urban Wildland*. Houghton Mifflin, Boston, Massachusetts.

Razani, N., Hills, N., Thompson, D. and Rutherford, G. (2020) The association of knowledge, attitudes and access with park use before and after a park-prescription intervention for low-income families in the U.S. *International Journal of Environmental Research and Public Health* 13(3): 701.

Richmond, D., Sibthorp, J. and Wilson, C. (2019) Understanding the role of summer camps in the learning landscape: an exploratory sequential study. *Journal of Youth Development* 14(3), 9–30.

Rueben, A. (2019) Science's newest miracle drug is free. *Outside Magazine* 1 May. Available at: https://www.outsideonline.com/2393660/science-newest-miracle-drug-free (accessed 23 December 2020).

Schuttler, S., Sorensen, A., Jordan, R., Cooper, C. and Shwartz, A. (2018) Bridging the nature gap: can citizen science reverse the extinction of experience? *Frontiers in Ecology and the Environment* 16(7), 405–411.

Shiva, V. (2016) *Staying Alive: Women, Ecology, and Development*. North Atlantic Books, Berkeley, California.

Sibthorp, J., Paisley, K. and Gookin, J. (2007) Exploring participant development through adventure-based programming: a model from the National Outdoor Leadership School. *Leisure Sciences* 29(1), 1–18.

Simpson, L. (2004) Anticolonial strategies for the recovery and maintenance of Indigenous knowledge. *The American Indian Quarterly* 28(3), 373–384.

Soga, M. and Gaston, K.J. (2016) Extinction of experience: the loss of human–nature interactions. *Frontiers in Ecology and the Environment* 14(2), 94.

Soga, M., Yamanoi, T., Tsuchiya, K., Koyanagi, T.F. and Kanai, T. (2018) What are the drivers of and barriers to children's direct experiences of nature? *Landscape and Urban Planning* 180, 114–120.

Swimme, B. and Berry, T. (1992) *The Universe Story*. Arkana Publishing, London.

Tanja-Dijkstra, K., Pahl, S., White, M.P., Auvray, M., Stone, R.J., *et al.* (2018) The soothing sea: a virtual coastal walk can reduce experienced and recollected pain. *Environment and Behavior* 50(6), 599–625.

Warfield, H.A. (2018) From existential to ideological communitas: can pilgrimage connect and transform the world? In: Warfield, H. and Hetherington, K. (eds) *Pilgrimage as Transformative Process*. Brill Rodopi, Boston, Massachusetts, pp. 33–42.

White, M., Yeo, N., Vassiljev, P., Lundstedt, R., Wallergård, M., *et al.* (2018) A prescription for "nature": the potential of using virtual nature in therapeutics. *Neuropsychiatric Disease and Treatment* 14, 3001–3013.

Whyte, K.P. (2013) On the role of traditional ecological knowledge as a collaborative concept: a philosophical study. *Ecological Processes* 2(1): 7.

Wong, G., Ng, T., Lee, J., Lim, P., Chua, S., *et al.* (2020) Horticultural therapy reduces biomarkers of immunosenescence and inflammaging in community-dwelling older adults: a feasibility pilot randomized controlled trial. *The Journals of Gerontology: Series A Biological Sciences and Medical Sciences* 76(2): glaa271.

Zarr, R., Wells, A. and Wolf, K. (2020) Park Rx [Webinar]. *Shift Health and Nature webinar series*, 14 July. Available at: https://shiftjh.org/the-health-nature-webinar-series/ (accessed 23 December 2020).

7　Connecting with Landscapes: Intentional Access to Green Space

> The hunger for trees is outspoken and seemingly universal. Landscaping should be as essential a part of the basic infrastructure of a settlement as electricity, water, sewers and paving.
> ~Kevin Lynch (1918–1984), author and urban planner

To experience the health-promoting aspects of landscapes and maintain healthy relationships with the natural world, one must have access. The process of urbanization and industrialization has generally decreased the amount and quality of nature that people encounter in their daily lives. Strategies such as creating protected areas like parks and reserves and introducing various forms of urban green space and blue space can help. Valuing practices and spaces such as these is beneficial to human and planetary well-being. This is more essential than ever in the face of continuing urbanization, recognition of historic environmental injustice, pressing environmental issues brought about by climate change, and worsening healthcare crises. For example, mental illness constitutes a significant and growing disease burden worldwide (Rehm and Shield, 2019; Schumann et al., 2019), and Schumann et al. (2019) found environmental factors associated with urbanization are the most rapidly growing cause of mental illness, including increased prevalence of anxiety, depression, and substance abuse. If incorporating parks and other natural areas into development (a socioecological approach to well-being) makes a significant difference in public health, then policy makers and urban planners need this research to be available.

This chapter begins with a discussion of environmental narratives and the ways they shape our collective beliefs about natural landscapes, and then presents conservation and preservation ideas and strategies followed by a variety of approaches to integrating nature into the places and landscapes where people live.

Environmental Narratives

Worldviews impact the ways we perceive and experience natural spaces and how we construct environmental narratives. The dominant Western narrative and subsequent environmental discourse promotes estrangement from the natural world by constructing a false dichotomy between humans and nature. This fabricated separation is reinforced by what some scholars call the "fall-recovery narrative" where nature is understood to be in decline from a pristine state and needs to return to baseline (Dickinson, 2013). These narratives are detrimental because of the sense of estrangement they cause and because they obscure issues of environmental justice and power structures as they relate to natural landscapes. Dickinson (2013) argued that our sense of disconnection from nature is caused by "psychological, interpersonal and cultural fracturing," which reinforce the notion that nature is "out there," and that to heal, we need to go and find it. She argued that what we are currently experiencing is not a sudden falling away from nature in modern times, but rather a long history of cultural and

DOI: 10.1079/9781789245400.0007

psychological alienation. Thus, to fully understand the problem and find sustainable solutions, we need to understand the past.

In the USA, the dominant environmental narrative tells the story of settlers arriving from Europe to find pristine and untamed wilderness, which they then "conquered" in order to survive. In reality, there existed a vast network of Indigenous nations that utilized a wide range of sophisticated land management practices, including tending large-scale gardens, using fire to manage pastures and grazing lands, and implementing advanced agricultural techniques (Dunbar-Ortiz, 2014). Indigenous peoples maintained expansive road and trail systems, complex forms of governance, and effective medical and dental practices that allowed for a virtually disease-free population (prior to the spread of new diseases such as smallpox). While the landscapes encountered by the settler-colonialists were full of thriving nature, and even wild, these landscapes were not untouched or unimpacted by humans.

Two major differences between Indigenous cultures and those of the colonizers were the Eurocentric concept of private property and the ideal of wealth accumulation. In pursuit of these ideals, European colonizers used brutal tactics to forcibly remove Indigenous peoples from their lands and then abducted people from Africa to use as slaves to tend the newly acquired land and make it profitable. Among the settler-colonialists, and arising from dominant European worldviews of the time, **wilderness**[1] was considered a place to be feared and tamed, and the relationship with the land was predominantly adversarial and extractive. One of the consequences of the **culture of conquest** (Dunbar-Ortiz, 2014) of the settler-colonialists was the inevitable destruction and pollution of the land. This happened rapidly during the industrial eras (see Chapter 2, this volume), though the path was paved long before.

Related information: What's in a name?

Part of the movement to reconcile historical narratives is born of the practice of reconsidering place names. In many colonized nations, places were renamed after the explorers who were said to discover or conquer the land (or mountain, river, etc.). This practice of erasure of Indigenous names serves to rewrite history in an ongoing way. One way of unraveling systems of oppression is to allow these places to retain the names given by their historical ancestors or to include those ancestors in the process of renaming. An example of this is the Gore Mountain Range in Western Colorado, which may soon be renamed the Nuchu Range (Blevins, 2020). This name, meaning "Ute's Range," was chosen by Ute tribal leaders. The organization Native Land Digital has created interactive maps of Indigenous territories and languages that can be accessed online and through smartphone apps. Using tools such as these, Indigenous and non-Indigenous people can improve their relationships with the land around them and work toward righting historical wrongs (Native Land Digital, n.d.).

Conservation and Preservation

The first industrial revolution in Europe and the USA prompted a mass migration of workers into heavily polluted metropolitan areas, leading to widespread health and social issues. In part as a foil to industrialization, the major art and literature movement of the time, romanticism, emphasized nature over industry. In the 1700s and 1800s, led by the romantic movement, "wilderness" began its transformation from a place of fear and hostility to a place of health, restoration, adventure, and respite from life in the cities (Nash, 2014). The writers, adventurers, and artists who led this movement were mostly city dwellers, who enjoyed the luxuries of money, time, and lifestyles generally free from manual labor. Their ability to extoll the virtues of nature left a lasting impression, especially on the settler-colonialists of the relatively new USA. The wilderness became something of a national icon, infusing itself into the cultural fabric of a nation that had relatively little else to distinguish itself from the old world (Nash, 2014). These sentiments influenced well-known writers like Thoreau and Muir whose work seeded the conservation and preservation movement in the USA.

Conservation, or designating certain areas of land for protection, is generally considered to be a response to industrialization. Given the technology for rapid growth and development, settler-colonialists needed to balance the negative effects on the environment and rapid overuse of natural resources. Conservation, which is considered a "wise-use strategy," is sometimes distinguished from preservation, which attempts to entirely protect landscapes from consumption and intrusive development. An example of conservation is the United States Forest Service (USFS), which manages forests for both recreation and logging/resource extraction in a way that it deems sustainable. An example of preservation is the National Wilderness Preservation System, as defined and protected by the Wilderness Act of 1964, which designates specific areas of land to protect from all forms of mechanization, resource use, and development.

As a cultural adaptation, conservation and preservation practices have formalized a perceived separation between humans and natural landscapes, while attempting to balance ongoing access to and use of resources, such as timber or oil, with the protection of the natural environment as a whole. These policies have proved effective in protecting parts of the natural environment from unchecked destruction, but they have also had the effect of continuing the forced removal of native peoples from their land in an effort to protect and preserve an idealized version of "nature" that does not include human inhabitants. There is great value in the protection of the natural environment from development and other forms of destruction, but we must simultaneously recognize the harm that these strategies have inflicted through the marginalization and displacement of people over time. Understanding the complete history of these lands (and not just the stories the dominant culture chooses to reify) helps us to create solutions that benefit the health of a wider diversity of people and the planet.

In 1832, Arkansas Hot Springs Reservation became the first US reserve, setting a precedent for governmental protection of land. This was followed throughout the 1800s and early 1900s by the establishment of US state and national parks, forests, monuments, and other land protection designations. Fueled by the industrialization and prosperity of the 1920s, people in North America began to travel to see these parks and preserves, prompting a culture of camping. Facilitated by the highway system and the advent of the personal automobile, more people were able to experience these natural wonders, though mostly from the wealthy classes. These personal experiences helped drive further legislation toward land protection in the USA and Canada.

This period was also marked by increased pollution in cities, leading to a national grappling with the importance of natural landscapes for health. One outcome of this was the development of Central Park in New York City, first proposed in the 1840s in response to the rapidly increasing population and the resultant crowding, noise, and chaos of city life. Construction began in 1857, and Central Park has become a thriving and iconic city park, with over 42 million visitors annually. Another example, the Appalachian Trail—a linear span of wildlands connecting Maine to Georgia—was envisioned by founder Benton MacKaye as a resource for citizens to access recreation, health, recuperation from illness, and as a means of creating jobs.

Public support for land protection has also emerged from rising interest in outdoor recreation and adventure sports. In the early 1800s, the concept of going to the mountains for health was becoming in vogue. By the 1820s, mountaineering and adventure pursuits as vacations were becoming popular in Europe, and by the 1930s, the British Mountaineering Leadership Scheme was developed. This beginning of exploration and adventure excursions formed the basis for adventure travel and later, adventure education programming and challenge course programs. Adventure education, outdoor education, and environmental education (see Chapter 6, this volume) differentiated into different fields in the 1970s, but they each utilized outdoor activities to encourage sense of place and a relationship with the natural world (Mitten et al., 2017). While these types of programs are typically associated with faraway wilderness-like settings, they can also be effectively practiced in urban environments. Urban adventure and environmental education programs are more accessible to people from a range of incomes and ethnic backgrounds and help people connect with nearby nature (Warren et al., 2014).

In the USA, four federal land management agencies—the USFS, the National Park Service (NPS), the Bureau of Land Management (BLM), and the United States Fish and Wildlife Service (USFWS)—oversee important conservation and preservation efforts and provide opportunities for recreation and connection to natural landscapes. Together, these agencies manage 614 million acres, or 26.6% of US land (Willoughby, 2018). In recent years, these federal agencies have embraced the role of parks and protected areas in health promotion, including the Healthy Parks Healthy People campaign of the NPS, and the More Kids in the Woods program of the USFS. However, much of this land is distant from many people's everyday lives, disproportionately concentrated in 11 western states and Alaska and requiring access to a private car or air travel, in addition to costs of entry, camping equipment, time away from work, and so on. Even for people able to negotiate these barriers, access to these spaces may only take place occasionally, on weekends or a few weeks a year during family vacations or road trips.

US state parks are one resource that many people rely on to access nature experiences closer to home. In 2020, there were 6792 state parks in the USA, with 813 million visitors (America's State Parks, 2020). There are even more local, municipal, or county parks, nature centers, greenways, and other forms of green or blue space. At all levels, parks and recreation programs are important partners in human health and well-being. Researchers are also interested in the concept of nearby nature, operationalized as the nature or green space near people's homes, including both private and public spaces (Cox et al., 2017).

Of course, conservation is not just a US phenomenon. The first national park in the world, Bogd Khan Uul, was actually established in Mongolia in 1778 and may have been informally protected since at least the 12th century (Whitten, 2009). Worldwide, protected and conserved areas are recognized for their contributions to global health and sustainability (United Nations Environment Programme (UNEP)–World Conservation Monitoring Centre (WCMC), International Union for Conservation of Nature (IUCN), and National Geographic Society (NGS), 2020). According to the UNEP, in 2020, there were more than 245,000 designated protected areas listed in the World Database on

Protected Areas, representing 15.2% of the earth's land surface and 7.4% of the oceans. In response to global recognition of the damaging effects of human activities on nature, the IUCN was established in 1948 and now operates in over 160 countries. This organization promotes sustainable development and protection of natural resources worldwide through the collaboration of governments, civil society organizations, and experts from all over the globe. IUCN recently established the Health and Well-Being Specialist Group, which recognizes the foundational influence of nature on human health and the role that parks, protected areas, and green spaces play in allowing humans to access those benefits. By promoting the related research, facilitating partnerships, and influencing policy, the working group aims to support nature-based solutions to global health and environmental issues.

Globally, protection of both marine and terrestrial environments has steadily increased between 1990 and 2018, and this growth is expected to continue (UNEP–WCMC, IUCN, and NGS, 2020). Still, not everyone has access to nature, and distribution is inequitable. Regular access and exposure to healthy/non-toxic natural landscapes for all people require intentionality and buy-in from community members, organizations, and leadership, including appropriate policy making. To develop and sustain healthy relationships with the natural world, people need access to healthy natural landscapes where they live. Given global patterns of residency, this means that we must be both creative and intentional in constructing spaces that are accessible, aesthetically pleasing, health promoting, and environmentally beneficial. In many cases, it is too late to simply preserve natural areas before development takes over (a strategy that has historically also resulted in human displacement). Instead, existing urban areas must be retrofitted to prioritize green space and create healthy natural landscapes that include human residents. Many such strategies exist and are being utilized in cities and countries around the world.

Green by Design

In the USA, intentional design to incorporate nature into parks and planned communities goes back at least to the 1860s. Frederick Law Olmsted (1822–1903), one of the landscape architects responsible for the planning and design of Central Park, believed in both a therapeutic and a mystical effect of the natural landscape upon people and considered beautiful scenery to be an effective therapy against mental disease and the health issues related to modernization. Olmsted developed sites in line with their intrinsic qualities, and many sites have stood the test of time, including Yosemite National Park, the Niagara Reservation in Niagara, New York, which became the first official US state park, as well as one of the country's first planned communities in Riverside, Illinois. His work can still be experienced at many university campuses, parks, arboretums, cemeteries, gardens, and estates across the USA and Canada. Olmsted is credited with being the first person to use the term **landscape architect** as a job title, though the English-language term landscape architecture dates back at least to Gilbert Laing Meason, a Scotsman, in 1828 (Waldheim, 2014). Landscape architecture deals with the relationship between built structures (architecture) and the environment (landscape) and, according to Waldheim, was developed as a response to social and environmental issues posed by urbanization.

In 1903, the first garden city was constructed in Letchworth, England, designed by Ebenezer Howard. Garden cities emphasized self-contained communities with controlled population densities and featured a garden in the center surrounded by a ring of green space. Many of Howard's ideas contributed to the development of urban and suburban planning. In the USA, the profession of planning developed its roots in the early 1900s. This movement toward policy and regulation gained increasing importance throughout the early to mid-1900s as populations continued to urbanize, with the majority of global citizens living in urban areas for the first time in 2007. By 2050, more than two-thirds of global citizens are expected in live in urban areas (Ritchie and Roser, 2019).

Urban green and blue spaces (UGBS), or the integration of natural elements in urban environments, can be a key strategy in improving the livability of cities, especially as urban densification continues to increase around the world. Residential proximity to green space has been linked to diminished all-cause mortality, small for gestational age (SGA) births, cardiovascular and respiratory diseases, cancers, mental stress, and other health conditions. Additionally, research confirms that parks and green spaces save healthcare dollars, such as Watt *et al.*'s (2018) research demonstrating a saving of £34 billion GBP (£30 per person) because of existing parks/green space. Aspects of the built environment, such as parks, are modifiable through urban planning processes, and studies show that these types of interventions potentially have more positive and lasting health impacts than interventions designed to change individual behaviors (Balmes, 2019).

In addition to promoting health and well-being, boosting creativity, and facilitating learning, UGBS also provide **ecosystem services** such as flood reduction, pollution mitigation, erosion control, and temperature regulation, and may also boost local economies and improve neighborhood safety (House *et al.*, 2016). For example, research demonstrates that natural landscapes can provide physical protective factors from storms and other disasters, such as mangrove protecting shorelines from hurricanes and tsunamis (Erftemeijer *et al.*, 2020). Green space proximity also confers benefit through air-quality improvement, including the mitigation of exposure to volatile organic compounds (Yeager *et al.*, 2020). Green space in high-density areas reduces the heat island effect, thereby reducing heat stress and associated morbidity (Balmes, 2019).

The World Health Organization (WHO) recommends a minimum of 9 m^2 of green space per individual and ideally up to 50 m^2 (Russo and Cirella, 2018). When equitably distributed and easily accessible by all members of a community, residents can access documented health-promotion benefits. A recent review proposed three main pathways through which UGBS benefits accrue: (i) reducing harm/**mitigation** (e.g. reduced exposure to air pollution, noise, and heat); (ii) restoring capacities/**restoration** (e.g. attention restoration or stress recovery); and (iii) building capacities/**instoration** (e.g. encouraging physical activity or facilitating social cohesion) (Markevych *et al.*, 2017). These authors indicated that UGBS is generally accepted to be beneficial to health, but greater clarity in research methodology is needed to better understand pathways, context, and other contributing factors, such as culture, climate, and geography.

UGBS interventions must be carefully designed and executed or they may harbor unintended ill effects, such as providing habitat for disease vectors like ticks and mosquitoes, reducing air quality through increased allergenic pollen, providing places where crime may occur (or increasing the fear/perception of crime), and displacing marginalized populations through increased property values and rents (Markevych *et al.*, 2017). This process of displacement driven by green amenities, known as **ecological, environmental, or green gentrification** (Anguelovski *et al.*, 2018), exacerbates problems related to social determinants of health. The solution to this issue is not less green space but rather more research-based knowledge and public support. Several authors have suggested the strategy of making an area "just green enough," with attention to both social and ecological sustainability in the process of creation (Wolch *et al.*, 2014). One important aspect of this process is to include stakeholders from the communities themselves in the process of conceptualization, design, construction, and maintenance (Harshaw, 2018).

Greening initiatives can contribute to the overall well-being of low-income residents through the creation of a green-collar workforce. One example of this is Sustainable South Bronx, founded in 2001 by Majora Carter, which provides paid training for environmental jobs to restore urban green spaces (e.g. constructing greenways and building green roofs), enabling residents to contribute to neighborhood health, combat environmental injustices, and gain meaningful future employment (Jennings *et al.*, 2017). The US-based Trust for Public Land (TPL) envisions a future where all citizens live within a 10-min walk to a park, a metric that is currently unmet by one in three citizens. In pursuit of this goal, TPL engages in fundraising, research, planning, advocacy, and design of parks, playgrounds, trails, and gardens, with an emphasis on health, equity, and climate resilience.

Many different approaches prioritize the incorporation of nature into urban/suburban living, depending on existing infrastructure, geography, space, and community priorities. Table 7.1 details some of these methods.

Table 7.1. Urban green and blue space (UGBS) approaches.

Approach	How nature is incorporated into urban and suburban living[a]
Biophilic design	Derived from the biophilia hypothesis, this design philosophy emphasizes incorporation of elements, systems, and processes from the natural world into the built environment. The proponents of biophilic design recognize the health-promoting aspects of contact with nature and the potential for modern environments to both degrade and alienate us from nature (Kellert, 2018). Kellert and Calabrese (2015) identified three biophilic design categories: (i) direct experience of nature, which includes elements such as sunlight, water, plants, natural landscapes, air, and so on; (ii) indirect experiences of nature, which includes attributes such as images of nature, natural materials and colors, simulating/evoking nature, natural geometries, shapes and forms, and so forth; and (iii) experience of space and place, which includes attributes such as prospect and refuge, organized complexity, and cultural and ecological place attachment. Taken together, these experiences and attributes may help designers create spaces that enable connection to the natural environment and promote health and well-being.
Compact cities	The presence of UGBS has been recognized as being particularly important in the design of **compact cities**, which are characterized by high density and a mixed-use pattern, allowing for both functional design and sustainability (Russo and Cirella, 2018). A number of existing cities provide notable examples of this type of design, including Singapore, Chicago, and Ljubljana, Slovenia, the 2016 European Green Capital. In Hong Kong—a compact city with over 40% of the territory in protected areas and open space—schools offer urban adventure education opportunities, where students learn about their surroundings, increase sense of place and belonging, and learn about conservation (Mitten *et al.*, 2017).

Continued

Table 7.1. Continued.

Approach	How nature is incorporated into urban and suburban living[a]
Greenways	Greenways are corridors of land, typically containing a trail (paved or unpaved) that link people and places together. Greenways may follow rivers or streambeds, abandoned railroad beds, utility corridors, or other linear open space. They provide ecosystem services while encouraging physical activity and recreation, providing alternative forms of transportation, enhancing community identity, and boosting economic activity and property values (Lindsey *et al.*, 2004). Greenways, especially those with paved paths, can be accessible to a wide variety of users. In the USA, organizations such as the Rails-to-Trails Conservancy are generating research and advocacy toward the investment in and construction of more trails for transportation, recreation, and environmental protection.
Natural playgrounds	Natural playgrounds remove traditional play structures like swings and slides, which have prescribed uses and limit creativity, and replace them with natural elements like logs, stumps, rocks, and sand, which encourage creative interaction such as climbing and building. These types of playgrounds encourage cooperative play, healthy risk taking, and hands-on interaction with natural elements, as well as safe and comfortable transitions from indoor or playground areas to wild natural areas. Similar ideas include "nature explore classrooms," nature discovery areas, loose parts play, and natural playscapes.
Pocket parks	Pocket parks are small parks, typically the size of one to four house lots, and serve approximately a 0.4 km (¼ mile) radius, providing small-scale, accessible green spaces to nearby residents and workers (Kronkosky Charitable Foundation, 2016). These parks present an opportunity for collaboration between residents of an area and government officials to convert unused spaces and vacant lots into ecologically beneficial areas that also support the health and well-being of community members. Local citizens can be empowered to create their own green spaces, with the help of local foundations/ organizations and funding from agencies such as the TPL. Many of these spaces are utilized as community gardens, providing another tangible benefit in the form of local food. Careful planning is required, but pocket parks can be highly successful due to their responsiveness to local community needs.
Rooftop gardens/ green roofs	Rooftop gardens, also called green roofs, have been shown to have a number of economic and environmental benefits, including increased property values, improved stormwater management, reduced urban heat island effects and improved air quality, insulation of the building (leading to reduced heating/ cooling costs, improved mechanical efficiency, and diminished noise), reduced greenhouse gas emissions, extended roof life and provision of urban amenities such as pleasant views, spaces for recreation, wildlife habitat, and food production (National Park Service, n.d.).
Therapeutic gardens	Designed with intentionality toward therapeutic benefits to visitors, a "therapeutic garden" is a specific designation from the AHTA, which also draws on best practices from other organizations including the American Society of Landscape Architects. These gardens are often found in healthcare, rehabilitative, and other therapeutic settings and according to the AHTA have seven characteristics: (i) scheduled and programmed activities; (ii) features modified to improve accessibility; (iii) well-defined perimeters; (iv) a profusion of plants and plant–people interactions; (v) benign and supportive conditions

Continued

Table 7.1. Continued.

Approach	How nature is incorporated into urban and suburban living[a]
	(e.g. avoidance of pesticides and provision of shade/shelter); (vi) universal design (e.g. accommodate people of all ages and abilities); and (vii) recognizable placemaking (Hazen, 2013). These spaces work in conjunction with horticultural therapy programs (see Chapter 6, this volume) to achieve their full potential.
Urban gardens	Urban gardening is simply the practice of growing food or other plants in urban environments. These gardens can be found on rooftops, balconies, small lots, or even vertically on building walls. Urban gardening is currently enjoying a resurgence in popularity, though the idea reaches back to ancient civilizations. As a form of food security, urban gardens became especially popular in the USA in response to food shortages and quarantine directives during the COVID-19 pandemic, mirroring the historical practice of planting victory gardens during World Wars I and II (Garrity, 2020). Inequitable access to healthy food is characteristic of many low-income cities in the USA. In these areas, sometimes referred to as food apartheid (a term that is replacing "food desert" to signify that the problem is not geographical but rather created by systems of inequity), community gardens can provide access to nutritious food while promoting social and environmental bonds within one's community and providing opportunity for physical activity (Jennings *et al.*, 2017).

[a] AHTA, American Horticultural Therapy Association; COVID-19, coronavirus disease 2019; TPL, Trust for Public Land. Bold text indicates a new term.

It is important to note the potentially vast heterogeneity between different UGBS of the same type. For example, an urban garden could be a few pots on a balcony, an expansive rooftop garden providing recreational as well as food security benefits, or a small swath of otherwise undeveloped land. This diversity may partially account for the mixed results of some research studies, where findings may be difficult to replicate or are even contradictory (e.g. Dallimer *et al.*, 2012). Instead of focusing on *type* of space, Hunter and Luck (2015) suggested a typology of green space *qualities* (e.g. physical attributes, access, management/ownership), arguing that the specific social and ecological qualities of a space interact to create social–ecological values. Focusing on these values may help researchers focus less on quantities of green space and more on importance, worth, or usefulness of these areas. These authors provide the example of a sports field and a botanic garden; both may contribute positively to health but in different ways and for different populations. Focusing research on green space qualities and associated socioecological values may help researchers to better ascertain the benefits of UGBS through more accurate measurements and reduction of confounding variables. These qualities highlight the socioecological nature of landscapes where humans both impact and are impacted by their environments.

China: Wellness tourism focuses on interaction with natural landscapes
By Haoai Zhao

China is a land of great diversity, in part due to its large territory, around 9.6 million km^2 with 18,000 km of coastline. In China, wellness tourism has developed rapidly in recent decades (Voigt and Pforr, 2013). People in China travel to destinations looking for natural environments that they believe will offer benefits to their mental health, physical health, and longevity.

In the early centuries, people in ancient China believed that nature had a mysterious power, which produced medicinal herbs, magical fruits, minerals, and imagined animals that promised longevity. In Chinese mythology, these magical herbs, fruits, minerals, and imagined animals are always hidden in the mountains, forests, oceans, caves, and grottoes that humans can hardly reach. The early Chinese philosophy toward nature was deeply rooted in the belief system of Chinese people, and it is part of the foundation of Chinese culture.

People traveling to destinations with motivations for wellness is common in China. One example is China's Bama Yao Autonomous County, which has attracted numerous tourists for the quality of its natural environment and reputation for longevity (Huang and Xu, 2014). Bama County is located in the north-west part of the Guangxi Zhuang Autonomous Region in China. It was once one of the poorest counties in China and perceived as a marginal place. The karst landscape and mild weather, however, make Bama a beautiful place to stay. The place is surrounded by abundant natural landscapes such as mountains, rivers, forests, and caves. Bama has a high percentage of centenarians in China, which makes it attractive to people, especially those with chronic diseases. The majority of wellness tourists in Bama are repeat visitors who stay for at least 1 month each year (Huang and Xu, 2018). Many of these visitors believe that Bama's good natural environment is the key to staying healthy. People stay in Bama for fresh air, clean water, food, and beautiful natural landscapes that they believe could keep them healthy or even remove illness from them.

In modern China, traditional health beliefs are still widely accepted and practiced by Chinese people. For example, people try to balance the yin and yang in the body by exchanging qi with the external natural landscape. "Sand therapy" is one of the traditional healthcare means inherited by the Uyghur people in Xinjiang, China (Abuduguli and Pataer, 2014) and was listed as a national-level intangible cultural heritage in 2014. In this practice, the desert becomes a therapeutic space for people with physical illness. People use this natural therapy to treat rheumatism, arthritis, and other chronic diseases that feature pain in the legs, hands, back, and wrists (Saidula *et al.*, 2011). Turpan, also known as the "fiery land" is the best-known place for sand therapy. Turpan's weather in summer can reach 48°C, and the sand temperature under the surface at 10 cm is 60°C. In this unique physical environment, people bury their bodies under the sand for 10–15 min to obtain healing.

In Chinese culture, people not only take materials (e.g. herbs, minerals, fruits) from nature but also use different methods to build spiritual relationships with nature. People try to obtain healing effects through their spiritual connection to nature. In traditional Chinese philosophy, 天人合一 (tian-ren-he-yi) has a great impact on Chinese people's view on health. 天人合一 (tian-ren-he-yi) means that nature and humans are united as a whole.

Socioecological Approach to Human Health

A socioecological approach to human health is an attempt at a true integration of science, societal needs, and ideology. As early as 1986, the WHO proclaimed that healthcare is not separate from caring for the environment. The Ottawa Charter for Health

Promotion, created in 1986 at the first international conference on health promotion in Ontario, Canada, called for a socioecological approach to health management, including environmental protection in the name of health reform (Public Health Agency of Canada, 2008). Achieving health equity, or the "attainment of the highest level of health for all people" (Jennings *et al.*, 2017, p. 2), is a critical issue in the USA and abroad. The traditional approach to achieving this goal has been to improve access to medical care. While undeniably important, this strategy has ignored other health disparities related to race, class, and political power. Improving social and physical environments is a key pathway to improving health equity (Jennings *et al.*, 2017). This includes the maintenance of quality green spaces, which are related to a number of social determinants of health, including education, neighborhood and built environment, and economic stability.

A socioecological approach emphasizes an interwoven relationship between people and their environment, connecting public policy (and policy makers), community structures, organizations, individuals, and landscapes. As disciplines begin to overlap and policy makers from environmental, public health, recreation, psychology, landscape architecture, medical, and urban planning backgrounds collaborate, a truer understanding of the need, potential, and practice of socioecological approaches to health management and promotion results.

Natural landscapes, including public-owned parks, play a key role in a socioecological approach to health because these environments encourage and enable people to relate to each other and the natural world (Maller *et al.*, 2006). Incorporating natural landscapes into an overall health plan for people was the approach that Olmsted and others used in park and green space development. All people, but especially those in urban environments, need natural areas maintained in close proximity to their living spaces to experience the benefits of a healthy relationship with the natural world.

Conclusion

Humans have a long history of modifying their landscapes and environments. This process influences the ways we connect to landscape and how landscapes influence our health and well-being. Over time, the influence of technology and changing worldviews have led to industrialization, modernization, and urbanization throughout the world. Simultaneously, worldviews about the natural environment have changed, leading to the protection of natural spaces for reasons ranging from tourism and recreation to environmental preservation. The protection of the natural environment remains a critical goal to ensure the health of our planet and all its inhabitants, but it must be done in sustainable and life-affirming ways that emphasize our interconnectedness rather than attempting to draw boundaries between humans and nature.

People from many disciplines have an opportunity to bring nature and people together in forms that can be experienced through everyday life. Simultaneously, we can continue to protect larger conservation areas in ways that are socially just, helping to combat global warming while protecting ways of life, Indigenous knowledge, and human dignity. The future of our planet depends on acting both locally and globally while helping individual people access a sense of connection to the natural world that translates to action to safeguard it for future generations.

Note

[1] Scholars argue that, in fact, the "new world" was not wilderness at all, and if it had been, the colonialists would not have been able to survive as they lacked the necessary skills and knowledge.

References

Abuduguli, A. and Pataer, H. (2014) The introduction of sand therapy of traditional U Medicine. *Journal of Medicine & Pharmacy of Chinese Minorities* 20(1), 71–72.

America's State Parks (2020) Get to Know America's State Parks. Available at: https://www.stateparks.org/about-us/ (accessed 28 January 2021).

Anguelovski, I., Connolly, J.J., Masip, L. and Pearsall, H. (2018) Assessing green gentrification in historically disenfranchised neighborhoods: a longitudinal and spatial analysis of Barcelona. *Urban Geography* 39(3), 458–491.

Anon (1964) *Wilderness Act of 1964*. 16 U.S.C. 1131–1136, 78 Stat. 890. United States of America.

Balmes, J.R. (2019) Greening of the heart and mind. *Journal of the American Heart Association* 8(6): e012090. doi: 10.1161/JAHA.119.012090.

Blevins, J. (2020) George Gore's bloody legacy could soon be erased from Colorado's mountains, replaced with a nod to the Utes. *The Colorado Sun* 18 September. Available at: https://colorado-sun.com/2020/09/18/changing-gore-to-nuchu-ute-range/ (accessed 29 December 2020).

Cox, D.T., Shanahan, D.F., Hudson, H.L., Fuller, R.A., Anderson, K., *et al.* (2017) Doses of nearby nature simultaneously associated with multiple health benefits. *International Journal of Environmental Research and Public Health* 14(2): 172.

Dallimer, M., Irvine, K., Skinner, A., Davies, Z., Rouquette, J., *et al.* (2012) Biodiversity and the feel-good factor: understanding associations between self-reported human well-being and species richness. *BioScience* 62(1), 47–55.

Dickinson, E. (2013) The misdiagnosis: rethinking "nature-deficit disorder". *Environmental Communication: a Journal of Nature and Culture* 7(3), 315–335.

Dunbar-Ortiz, R. (2014) *An Indigenous peoples' history of the United States*. Beacon Press, Boston, Massachusetts.

Erftemeijer, P.L., Agastian, T., Yamamoto, H., Cambridge, M.L., Hoekstra, R., *et al.* (2020) Mangrove planting on dredged material: three decades of nature-based coastal defence along a causeway in the Arabian Gulf. *Marine and Freshwater Research* 71(9), 1062–1072.

Garrity, A. (2020) Victory gardens are making a comeback amid coronavirus food shortage fears. *Good Housekeeping* 13 May. Available at: https://www.goodhousekeeping.com/home/gardening/a32452189/what-is-a-victory-garden-coronavirus-pandemic/ (accessed 29 December 2020).

Harshaw, P. (2018) Do parks push people out? *Bay Nature Magazine* 1 October. Available at: https://baynature.org/article/do-parks-push-people-out/ (accessed 16 May 2021).

Hazen, T. (2013) Therapeutic garden characteristics. *A Quarterly Publication of the American Horticultural Therapy Association* 41(2): 3.

House, E., O'Connor, C., Wolf, K., Israel, J. and Reynolds, T. (2016) *Outside Our Doors: the Benefits of Cities Where People and Nature Thrive*. The Nature Conservancy, Washington State Chapter, Washington, DC.

Huang, L. and Xu, H. (2014) A cultural perspective of health and wellness tourism in China. *Journal of China Tourism Research* 10(4), 493–510.

Huang, L. and Xu, H. (2018) Therapeutic landscapes and longevity: wellness tourism in Bama. *Social Science & Medicine* 197, 24–32.

Hunter, A.J. and Luck, G.W. (2015) Defining and measuring the social-ecological quality of urban greenspace: a semi-systematic review. *Urban Ecosystems* 18(4), 1139–1163.

Jennings, V., Baptiste, A.K., Jelks, O. and Skeete, R. (2017) Urban green space and the pursuit of health equity in parts of the United States. *International Journal of Environmental Research and Public Health* 14(11): 1432.

Kellert, S.R. (2018) *Nature by Design: the Practice of Biophilic Design*. Yale University Press, New Haven, Connecticut.

Kellert, S. and Calabrese, E. (2015) *The Practice of Biophilic Design*. Terrapin Bright LLC, London.

Kronkosky Charitable Foundation (2016) Pocket Parks Research Brief. March, 1–4. Available at: https://kronkosky.org/Research/Foundation-Research/Research-Briefs (accessed 29 December 2020).

Lindsey, G., Man, J., Payton, S. and Dickson, K. (2004) Property values, recreation values, and urban greenways. *Journal of Park and Recreation Administration* 22(3), 69–90.

Maller, C., Townsend, M., Pryor, A., Brown, P. and St Leger, L. (2006) Healthy nature healthy people: 'contact with nature' as an upstream health promotion intervention for populations. *Health Promotion International* 21(1), 45–54.

Markevych, I., Schoierer, J., Hartig, T., Chudnovsky, A., Hystad, P., *et al.* (2017) Exploring pathways linking greenspace to health: theoretical and methodological guidance. *Environmental Research* 158, 301–317.

Mitten, D., Cheung, L., Yan, W. and Withrow-Clark, R. (2017) Adventure education. In: Russ, A. and Krasny, M. (eds) *Urban Environmental Education Review*. Cornell University Press. Ithaca, New York.

Nash, R. (2014) *Wilderness and the American Mind*, 5th edn. Yale University Press, New Haven, Connecticut.

National Park Service (n.d.) *Green Roof Benefits*. Technical Preservation Services, National Park Service US Department of the Interior. Available at: https://www.nps.gov/tps/sustainability/new-technology/green-roofs/benefits.htm (accessed 23 December 2020).

Native Land Digital (n.d.) Why It Matters. Native Land Digital. Available at: https://native-land.ca/about/why-it-matters/ (accessed 23 December 2020).

Public Health Agency of Canada (2008) *Ottawa Charter for Health Promotion*. Public Health Agency of Canada, Government of Canada, Ottawa. Available at: http://www.phac-aspc.gc.ca/ph-sp/docs/charter-chartre/index-eng.php (accessed 23 December 2020).

Rehm, J. and Shield, K.D. (2019) Global burden of disease and the impact of mental and addictive disorders. *Current Psychiatry Reports* 21(2), 10.

Ritchie, H. and Roser, M. (2019) Urbanization. Our World in Data. Available at: https://ourworldindata.org/urbanization (accessed 23 December 2020).

Russo, A. and Cirella, G.T. (2018) Modern compact cities: how much greenery do we need? *International Journal of Environmental Research and Public Health* 15(10): 2180.

Saidula, A., Yasheng, W. and Kuerban, S. (2011) Features and mechanisms of sand therapy. *Journal of Medicine & Pharmacy of Chinese Minorities* 17(9), 54–56.

Schumann, G., Benegal, V., Yu, C., Tao, S., Jernigan, T., *et al.* (2019) Precision medicine and global mental health. *The Lancet Global Health* 7(1): e32.

United Nations Environment Programme (UNEP)–World Conservation Monitoring Centre (WCMC), International Union for Conservation of Nature (IUCN), and National Geographic Society (NGS) (2020) *Protected Planet Live Report*. UNEP–WCMC, IUCN, and NGS, Cambridge, UK, Gland, Switzerland and Washington, DC.

Voigt, C. and Pforr, C. (eds) (2013) *Wellness Tourism: a Destination Perspective*. Routledge, New York.

Waldheim, C. (2014) Introduction: landscape as architecture. *Studies in the History of Gardens & Designed Landscapes* 34(3), 187–191.

Warren, K., Roberts, N.S., Breunig, M. and Alvarez, M.A.T.G. (2014) Social justice in outdoor experiential education: a state of knowledge review. *Journal of Experiential Education* 37(1), 89–103.

Watt, W., Lawton, R. and Fujiwara, D. (2018) *Revaluing Parks and Green Spaces: Measuring their Economic and Wellbeing Value to Individuals*. Fields in Trust, London.

Whitten, T. (2009) Mongolia: Tough Decisions About the World's Oldest Nature Reserve. World Bank Blogs, 28 April. Available at: https://blogs.worldbank.org/eastasiapacific/mongolia-tough-decisions-about-the-worlds-oldest-nature-reserve (accessed 23 December 2020).

Willoughby, S. (2018) Public Lands: Our Industry, Our Issue, Our Fight. What Are (and What Aren't) Public Lands? Outdoor Industry Association, 3 July. Available at: https://outdoorindustry.org/article/public-lands-industry-issue-fight-arent-public-lands/ (accessed 23 December 2020).

Wolch, J.R., Byrne, J. and Newell, J.P. (2014) Urban green space, public health, and environmental justice: the challenge of making cities 'just green enough'. *Landscape and Urban Planning* 125, 234–244.

Yeager, R., Riggs, D.W., DeJarnett, N., Srivastava, S., Lorkiewicz, P., *et al.* (2020) Association between residential greenness and exposure to volatile organic compounds. *Science of the Total Environment* 707: 135435.

8 Conclusions and Desired Future: Take a Park, Not a Pill

> We are part of everything that is beneath us, above us, and around us. Our past is our present, our present is our future, and our future is seven generations past and present.
> ~Winona LaDuke, environmentalist, political activist, and enrolled with the Ojibwe Nation

Throughout this book, we have asserted the importance of healthy relationships with natural landscapes for individual, community, and planetary health. We began by discussing what constitutes a natural landscape, the history of the human–natural landscape interface, the importance of worldviews, and the theoretical underpinnings that frame our understanding of these topics. We then explored the trajectory of related research, highlighting some of the outcomes and benefits conferred by natural landscapes, as well as applications and design considerations to help remedy our estrangement from the natural world. A valid critique of research about natural landscapes is the tendency to marginalize or stereotype Black, Indigenous and People of Color (BIPOC) communities. BIPOC contributions to our understanding and sense of connection to nature are essential. Issues of injustice, including those related to health, environment, and race, are interrelated; our capacity for empathy toward diverse peoples and cultures, and all living things, is a critical part of healing ourselves and the earth.

In this chapter, we consider the evidence underlying the assertion that natural landscapes are mutualistically-interwined with human health, and ask what constitutes a desired future, address the health-related needs and aspirations of many societies, and emphasize the role of natural landscapes in facilitating those desires. We support the importance of natural landscapes by discussing how the development of a land ethic and its corresponding concept of environmental responsibility is vital to human health. We conclude with a set of guiding principles intended to assist individuals and groups to act on information in this book.

Research-supported outcomes of spending time in or viewing nature include myriad social, physical, psychological, emotional, cognitive, and spiritual benefits (see Figure 5.3, Chapter 5, this volume). This body of research is helpful as we consider the needs and aspirations of society, and how these needs can be met through providing specific experiences in natural landscapes, and ensuring access to those landscapes via policy and design. These positive health effects may be overlooked, however, in light of negative perceptions held toward natural settings, sometimes labeled ecophobia (Estok, 2018). For many, natural settings may bring to mind natural disasters, dangerous animals, wildfires, and other events that can be injurious to people. Integrating nature-based experiences into everyday life, such as in schools, hospitals, and urban greening initiatives, may empower people to transcend their discord from the natural environment.

Without a healthy relationship with natural landscapes, people are unlikely to receive many of the benefits described in this book. Developing this relationship hinges on several factors:

- existence of and access to healthy natural environments;
- worldviews that support healthy relationships and prioritize protection of the earth over consumption and domination;

 DOI: 10.1079/9781789245400.0008

- programs and ideas that facilitate healthy relationships, teach outdoor skills, and provide opportunities for positive connection with the natural world; and
- efforts to repair historical injustices and include marginalized populations.

Because we are part of nature and nature is part of us, attention to the natural world is implicated in everything we do.

Research and Evidence: Considerations for the Future

International research from diverse fields ranging from medicine to recreation suggests that the benefits of exposure to nature are both pervasive and generalizable (Keniger *et al.*, 2013; Ewert *et al.*, 2014; Mygind *et al.*, 2019) and include numerous beneficial effects in health promotion and recovery from a broad range of diseases and ailments. However, research-related questions still remain. Attention to these questions may enable us to be more confident in the belief that healthy interactions with and care of natural landscapes can promote positive health outcomes, which may influence the adoption of policies and other related community or societal efforts.

1. People may perceive improved health from exposure to natural landscapes, but are they actually healthier?

While it is important for people to feel healthy, from a policy development perspective, it is crucial to know that they actually become healthy. Large-scale epidemiological studies enable researchers to circle back to a systems view and develop ways to work with nature while collecting more robust data. This approach, combined with advancing data collection methods and technologies, is beginning to help answer this question.

One example is the Green Heart Project in Louisville, Kentucky, and the associated HEAL study. In this experiment, researchers are planting thousands of trees and assessing health of residents on several metrics, including lifestyle choices (physical activity), social cohesion, and risk for heart disease and diabetes, as well as levels of air pollution, before and after the planting. Louisville is currently losing around 54,000 trees a year and has received an "F" in air-quality ratings from the American Lung Association every year since 2012. Researchers hope that this study will improve quality of life for Louisville residents and provide a validated "greenprint" that can be replicated in future cities. This study began in 2018 and is expected to conclude data collection in 2022.

The HEAL study builds on a 2018 study published in the *Journal of the American Heart Association* that provides direct evidence of physiological changes related to residential green space, suggesting that living in green neighborhoods could reduce cardiovascular disease risk because of decreased stress and an increased capacity for the body to repair blood vessels (Yeager *et al.*, 2018). One of the senior authors of the study, Aruni Bhatnagar, believes that these findings "support the transformation of urban greenness from a pleasant nicety to an essential health requirement" (Weaver, 2019). This research demonstrates the protective role natural landscapes play in health promotion and disease prevention.

2. What is the relationship between "naturalness" and health?

In other words, are certain types of natural landscapes more effective than others for promoting human health, and conversely, do urban environments consistently produce more negative outcomes? As discussed in Chapter 5, this volume, more nuanced research approaches are finding that people's responsiveness to scenery may conflate the distinction between urban and natural, with this response being impacted by factors such as the overall coherence of a particular scene. Some urban design strategies such as biophilic design (see Chapter 7, this volume) work to incorporate natural elements into the built environment and can include design aspects such as coherence that have been shown to promote restoration. Researchers and policy makers may also ask about differential effects of specific aspects of natural environments, such as the types of scenery, bodies of water, trees, or vegetation. For example, does moving water provide for a particularly restful and/or stress- or blood pressure-reducing outcome? If present, these differential effects can be considered in built environments. A related question is whether effects vary for different individuals and demographic groups, and if so, are there corresponding policy implications?

3. What kind of exposure to natural environments is needed to create a measurable effect?

Some research has focused on **dosage**—that is, the length and type of exposure to a natural landscape. For example, White *et al.*'s (2019) study suggested that spending at least 120 min a week in nature is associated with improved self-reported health and well-being. One strength of this study was its large and nationally representative sample (*n* = 19,806, weighted to be representative of the adult population of England). Findings were consistent across demographic categories, including gender, age, ethnicity, and area deprivation (greenness) and also accounted for people coping with long-term illness/disability, suggesting that the results were not simply due to healthier people visiting nature more often.

Using a scoping review, Meredith *et al.* (2020) found that 10 min or more of sitting or walking in various natural settings positively impacted defined psychological and physiological markers of mental well-being for college-aged individuals. In more specific research, D'Amore and Mitten (2014) found women's body image to be significantly better for women who spent 3 or more hours being active outside per week than for those who spent less than that. They also found that women who had participated in outside overnights as a child (e.g. at a 1- or 2-week summer camp) appeared to have significantly better body image as adults than those who had not, offering evidence of **durability** of experience.

Practitioners and researchers may also ask whether a particular experience is robust enough to be effective. For example, several adventure-based programs use natural environments to develop a sense of "hardiness" in military soldiers in an attempt to help them cope with issues such as post-traumatic stress disorder. Demonstrating the efficacy of experiences such as these may help garner structural support such as through medical insurance coverage, which may alleviate financial barriers to program participation and also support the organizations that provide programming.

4. What constitutes a "nature" experience? Does virtual nature count?

Virtual nature has been the subject of intensified research efforts because of its wide-ranging applicability and utility. Virtual nature and simulated natural landscapes can be useful in medical facilities, prisons, nursing homes, and other locations where "real" nature exposure might be impractical. Recent systematic reviews suggest that virtual nature experiences may be useful in altering certain mood states, but that more research is needed given the relatively small number of studies that currently exist (see Chapter 5, this volume).

If virtual nature experiences are effective, they should be utilized in ways that promote well-being while being cautious not to neglect the health benefits of visiting actual natural landscapes. The question of what is "real" nature is not new and is reflective of dominant society's propensity to view humans and human-made creations as separate from nature.

5. What are the roles of confounding variables and synergistic effects in explaining or amplifying the relationships between natural landscapes and health?

A **confounding variable** is another variable, other than those explicitly measured in a study, that has a hidden effect on study results. An example is related to correlational studies, such as those suggesting longer life expectancy is related to greenness (Gascon et al., 2016). Greener residential environments may be associated with high income levels (due to factors such as green gentrification and environmental racism); therefore, these results could be related to other factors conferred by high socioeconomic status, such as access to more nutritious food and better healthcare. Studies that demonstrate causation, such as the residential greenness studies mentioned above, may help researchers to tease apart these variables.

On the other hand, **synergistic effects** occur when two or more factors work together to create an even greater effect than the sum of each factor individually. For example, exercise outdoors may provide greater health benefit than comparable activity indoors because people tend to spend greater amounts of time outdoors (perhaps because exercise goals are incidental to other goals such as sightseeing or socialization) and because exposure to natural environments, even passively, has been shown to be beneficial to health (Mitten et al., 2016).

6. How can we work to ameliorate the issues of environmental injustice and environmental racism through research and associated policy making?

Research must consider how discrimination influences where people live and their access to natural areas. Structural racism and classism have a role in locating mining operations, toxic waste dumps, water control levees, and pipelines in BIPOC and low-income communities (Taylor, 2014; Wagner, 2020). People housed near these features have more limited access to clean outdoor landscapes. In other instances, after low-income urban areas become healthier environments through including more trees and other natural elements, gentrification often occurs (Maantay and Maroko, 2018). Beyond this, BIPOC communities have faced lack of funding support for parks and recreation areas, lack of representation in environmental jobs and mentorship, and more (see Chapter 6, this volume). Specific research addressing these issues can help practitioners provide more equity in access to programs, resources, and so on. Suárez *et al.* (2020) suggested three dimensions to address environmental justice: (i) distributive (fair distribution of ecosystem benefits); (ii) procedural (fairly integrating all affected peoples into the planning process); and (iii) recognition (incorporating the needs, values, and preferences of all groups).

7. How do changes in scientific understanding influence the questions we ask and our ability to come to new conclusions?

Scientific knowledge always evolves. Scientists and researchers use documented research procedures to arrive at a theory that is supported by evidence (see Chapters 4 and 5, this volume). Over time, as new information comes to light, other scientists may challenge an existing theory or build on it in ways that open up new research paths. Thus, theory change is a normal and healthy part of the scientific process. In some cases, this means that Western scientists are only beginning to "discover" what ancient cultures and Indigenous peoples have known for millennia. A diversity of perspectives ultimately bolsters our collective knowledge.

For example, many cultures have long known that humans are ecosystems and need healthy ecosystems to survive and thrive. Recent and promising scientific inquiry has focused on the **holobiont** concept, which refers to the combination of a host and its microbiota, such as humans and the gut flora so important to our digestive health. This concept is rooted in symbiosis research and studies the interactions between hosts and their microbial communities (Simon *et al.*, 2019). Moreover, this concept is an example of recent paradigm shifts in Western biology and carries implications for the health of humans, ecosystems, food production, and more.

Using a systems theory approach can help us think more globally to combine research findings in new ways. For example, research suggests a linkage between management of attention deficit hyperactivity disorder (ADHD) symptoms and greenness (Donovan *et al.*, 2019), as well as a linkage between ADHD symptoms and gut microbial diversity (Prehn-Kristensen *et al.*, 2018). A separate body of research looks at beneficial microbes, such as *Mycobacterium vaccae*, which is found in soil and is thought to have anti-inflammatory, immunoregulatory, and stress-resilience properties (Smith *et al.*, 2019). Perhaps microbial biodiversity plays a key role in the health-promoting effects of time spent in natural environments. More research exploring pathways such as this can potentially contribute to both healthcare savings and increased well-being.

Developing a Desired Future

Healthy natural landscapes are essential to well-being. While nature is not a panacea, time spent in natural landscapes is an important part of a larger constellation of health-related factors, including social determinants of health (SDOH), public policy, urban and suburban design, and individual lifestyle choices. Understanding the health-promoting aspects of the natural environment may function as one argument for its protection. Protecting the natural world solely for the benefit of human life (as we know it) on earth, however, is not enough. Without curbing consumption, recognizing the dignity of all humans, and honoring the value of all human and non-human lives, we will not succeed. We are at an inflection point regarding human relationships with the natural world. Variously referred to as the species moment, the great turning, the Anthropocene, and so on, the decisions we make now will impact future generations of humans, tigers, butter-flies, snails, trees, and every living organism. Global society is currently poised for change, making this a critical time to ask: What is our desired future?

The inherent complexity and uncertainty of future outcomes is challenging for any planning effort (Cameron and Potvin, 2016) and only exacerbated by the liminal nature of the present (see Chapter 2, this volume). A recent report from the National Academies of Sciences, Engineering, and Medicine (2019) suggested that the first step in developing a **desired future** involves helping people understand what a desired future might look like so they can discuss it, interact with others concerning its validity, and decide how to par-ticipate in its creation. Addressing factors such as landscape types and associated experi-ences, accessibility, management considerations, and integration into a human health paradigm can help communities co-create a desired future that fosters the collective health of both humans and natural landscapes.

A second step in developing a desired future is to account for different levels of indi-vidual commitment. Some people may be fully committed, believing that natural land-scapes are integral components for the promotion of positive health outcomes. Other people may have lower levels of commitment, perhaps valuing natural landscapes but not necessarily seeing them as related to their personal health. For others, the phenomena of racial and environmental injustice, such as green gentrification (see Chapter 7, this vol-ume), may lead to mistrust of policy makers and prompt people to elevate issues of sur-vival, such as being able to stay in their homes, over natural landscape concerns. Thus, experience in and availability of natural landscapes, as well as information concerning the connection between health and natural landscapes, may play a role in enhancing levels of commitment and helping people experience greater well-being.

Health needs and aspirations

We are currently experiencing global health crises of both people and the planet. According to the Centers for Disease Control (2020), the leading causes of death and dis-ability in the USA are chronic diseases, which affect six in ten adults. Global statistics are similar; the World Health Organization (WHO) reported that the top ten deadliest diseases worldwide in 2019 were: (i) ischemic heart disease; (ii) stroke; (iii) chronic obstructive pulmonary disease; (iv) lower respiratory infections; (v) neonatal conditions; (vi) respiratory cancers; (vii) Alzheimer's disease and dementia; (viii) dehydration from diarrheal diseases; (ix) diabetes; and (x) kidney diseases (WHO, 2020). Now COVID-19 will be on this list. Sedentary lifestyles and physical inactivity, a primary lifestyle risk for chronic diseases, contributed to an estimated 5.3 million premature deaths in 2008 (Lee *et al.*, 2012).

A systems approach recognizes the complex web of factors that contribute to these deaths. One of these factors—racism—was explicitly recognized as an "urgent public health threat" (para. 2) by the American Medical Association (AMA, 2020), emphasizing the role of systemic and structural racism in both health inequities and delivery of health-care. Climate change is another factor—an area that the WHO identifies as a top health challenge for the coming decade. Natural landscapes are not a panacea for solving the complicated issues of our time, but healthy natural landscapes have the potential to help heal both people and the planet.

SDOH underscore the importance of place (where people live, work, play, and learn) and related structural inequities that can be changed through policy making. For example, greater access to nature and open space in neighborhoods is related to better mental health in children, and the inequitable distribution of these spaces in neighborhoods is thought to be a key mechanism in perpetuating health inequity (Alderton *et al.*, 2019). These inequities impact how people experience natural landscapes, but they can also be mitigated by natural landscapes.

Japan: Mountains, the outdoors, and new challenges with COVID-19 By Aya Hayashi

Close to 70% of Japan comprises mountain and forest areas, and these natural landscapes have been very important to Japanese life. For ancient Japanese people, going to the mountains was a sacred religious activity. Mountains were the place where gods lived and where the souls of the dead traveled. For early Japanese culture, mountains represented a model of the universe, with high altitude and open spaces bearing names associated with heaven, and valleys, especially those with volcanic landforms, often called hell; the rivers between them connected both worlds. People expected their personalities to develop through receiving the grace of god in mountains (Hayashi, 2002).

Beginning in the early 20th century, a system of mountain huts opened to facilitate the experiences of hikers and climbers. This system contributes to the unique mountain culture and popularity of mountain climbing in Japan. In the 1980s, researchers at the Japanese Forestry Agency proposed *shinrin-yoku*, meaning forest bathing; this research-based health practice (see Chapter 5, this volume) has since spread to other countries and developed into forest therapy.

Since 2009, the number of people going to the mountains has doubled. In 2016, a new national holiday "Mountain Day" was set on 10 August to appreciate the blessing of mountains and natural environments. Motivations for going to the mountains vary, but a common reason is physical and mental health promotion. Yamamoto (2016) suggested four ways that natural landscapes impact human health: (i) long-term resistance exercise; (ii) expanding energy consumption; (iii) consuming fat; and (iv) mental and psychological benefits. In addition, in Japan, a number of psychologists and sociologists report health-related benefits such as refreshment, increased confidence, and bonding with groups. Using physiological and psychological measures on people mountain climbing in Japan, Hayashi *et al.* (2013) found a variety of benefits, including improvements in their immune systems and levels of hemoglobin, and an increased respiratory function.

In 2020, due to the spread of the COVID-19 virus in Japan and elsewhere, a variety of activity restrictions have been instituted. Even Mount Fuji, which is the highest mountain in Japan and climbed by more than 200,000 people every year, remained closed for the summer of 2020. Many of these restraints are due to the belief that high levels of use will
Continued

---

create higher infection rates and subsequent overload for medical workers. The restrictions are understandable for many outdoor people, but due to their close relationship with mountains, it is difficult to eliminate these activities from their daily lives. Therefore, there have been various ongoing endeavors to find new relationships with mountains and outdoor activities. Thus, what began in ancestral times as a belief that natural settings, such as mountains and forests, provided a place to attain a religious and spiritual experience has now become a quest for the promotion of personal health and safety.

The role of natural landscapes

Environments where people live can exert a tremendous influence on health. For example, Donovan *et al.* (2013) examined the influence of the loss of 100 million trees to the emerald ash borer, an invasive forest pest, on mortality rates. Because nature, or factors outside of the control of the investigators, governed people's exposure to the loss of neighborhood trees, the design arguably resembled random assignment, which strengthened the study. Results demonstrated an increase in mortality related to cardiovascular and lower respiratory tract illness in counties where trees were infested with the emerald ash borer. Across the 15 states in the study area, the borer was associated with an additional 6113 deaths related to illness of the lower respiratory system and 15,080 cardiovascular-related deaths. Research also suggested that people living in areas with greater amounts of forests, rangeland, or water exhibited longer life expectancies and higher levels of self-reported quality of life (Poudyal *et al.*, 2009).

Higher standards of living, impacted by race and class, often include greater access to natural areas such as greenways and open space. However, some research shows that green spaces may be **equigenic** or able to disrupt or partially mitigate inequity. Mitchell *et al.* (2015) found that inequalities in mental well-being among those with the best access to green space were about 40% less than those with the worst access. In other words, those with the greatest financial strain benefited the most from green space proximity. The presence of green space has been shown to decrease healthcare expenditures over time (see Chapter 7, this volume); therefore, attending to green space equity may lead to more social justice.

Engaging with natural landscapes—particularly experiences related to relaxation, reflection, aesthetic enjoyment, and physical activities such as walking—require a minimum of skill development or specialized equipment and have the potential to be accessible for a broad range of people (Mitten *et al.*, 2016). Attending to factors such as walkable access to nearby outdoor recreation areas (NORAs), or natural settings that are in close proximity to an individual's home or workplace, promotes accessibility and provides an effective healthcare cost saving (Watt *et al.*, 2018). Other strategies include incorporating natural landscapes into health-promotion plans, such as through park prescriptions and supporting grassroots organizations—particularly those with BIPOC leadership—in efforts to make outdoor culture more inclusive, and engaging with intentionally designed programs that may help facilitate a sense of connection to the outdoors (see Chapter 6, this volume).

Self-regulated restorative experiences (SRREs) are activities deliberately selected by individuals for the explicit purpose of providing recovery or restoration from the demands of everyday life (Degenhardt and Buchecker, 2012). Selecting specific restorative activities that can be done in NORAs can be an important component in overall well-being.

Some people lack the knowledge, skill, or social support to comfortably engage with natural landscapes on their own or develop their own SRREs. Intentionally designed outdoor experiences and programs can help. The disciplines of outdoor recreation and adventure education evolved in part as an answer to the estrangement many people felt from the natural world. Working in these fields, educators and guides plan and implement experiences that help people to acquire necessary knowledge and skills, provide equipment where necessary, and create social groups for these experiences. Many decades of related research showcase promising findings (see Chapters 5 and 6, this volume).

Desired and sought-after health-related outcomes are often linked to specific leisure and recreational activities, which may require specific types of natural landscapes. The Recreational Opportunity Spectrum is one tool for helping land managers link different landscapes with specific recreational activities (Clark and Stankey, 1979). For example, health outcomes that are influenced by social support and challenging physical activity may be achieved by participating in activities such as whitewater rafting, which requires a specific type of natural environment—namely, a whitewater river.

Land management strategies are increasingly recognized for their role in healthcare in both Western and non-Western approaches (Frumkin and Louv, 2007; Schultz *et al.*, 2018). A healthy environment translates to healthy people; thus, attending to the health and accessibility of natural landscapes should be an essential part of public health strategies and policy making. Equitable access to green space can benefit individual and community health, save healthcare dollars, disrupt inequity, provide ecosystem services, encourage tourism, and more.

Landscapes and policy making: developing a land ethic

In 1985, the US President's Commission on Americans Outdoors declared that the outdoors was a "giant health machine." This commission emphasized the role of natural landscapes in the well-being of the public, particularly through outdoor recreation activities, and provided specific recommendations and guidance for federal, state, local, public, and private policy making. Similar declarations have been made in other locations including the UK, Scandinavian countries, Australia, and Canada. With appropriate guidance from researchers and the public, policy making can play an important role in protecting the health of the environment and promoting health. Policy-related questions include: (i) the extent of available recreation resources; (ii) how land and facilities may change over time; (iii) staffing levels needed to meet demands; (iv) cooperation between federal, state, and local agencies and public and private land owners; (v) the prevention and resolution of resource conflicts; and (vi) the adequacy of laws, regulations, and policies (Siehl, 2008).

One outcome of the COVID-19 pandemic was overcrowding and destruction of iconic natural landscapes, simultaneously demonstrating the importance of these places and their vulnerability to human impact. Early 2020 also saw increased poaching of threatened and endangered species, accelerated deforestation, and other environmental pressures. We need more and healthier natural landscapes globally so that more people can enjoy them without damaging the ecosystems and without the negative consequences of driving people from their homes or forcing people to engage in destructive behaviors to survive. To accomplish this lofty but important goal, we must begin by rethinking the human–nature dichotomy so firmly engrained in dominant Western thought.

Dominant Western worldviews tend toward a transactional approach that emphasizes the ways humans can "use" natural landscapes to their benefit. This may benefit the health of some humans in the short term, but in the long term, this approach causes suffering for the health of people and the planet. Developing a land ethic is one alternative.

Aldo Leopold (1949) coined the term "land ethic" in his famous work, *A Sand County Almanac, and Sketches Here and There.* Leopold saw land as an enlargement of the community boundaries, such that the soil, plants, animals, and water are part of the human community rather than separate from it: "In short, a land ethic changes the role of *Homo sapiens* from conqueror of the land-community to plain member and citizen of it. It implies respect for his [*sic*] fellow-members, and also respect for the community as such" (Leopold 1949, p. 204). Leopold recognized that a conquering mentality was ultimately self-defeating, and that we were better off learning to work with the natural environment rather than trying to impose our will upon it. Thus, a land ethic meant learning to live in harmony with the land, as well as a willingness to sacrifice short-term economic gain for long-term environmental good.

A land ethic is an attempt to instill an ethic of care—to encourage people to act out of a sense of compassion and connectedness—rather than setting minimum environmental regulations and incentives based on rewards or punishments. As attributed to Maya Angelou, "I did then what I knew how to do. Now that I know better, I do better." (Oprah.com, 2011).

The life-giving natural environment can imbue immeasurable gifts of health—but only if we are able to provide reciprocal care and nurturance through our own sense of connection to the non-human natural world. Related philosophies and worldviews that emphasize the importance of developing a relationship with nature include traditional ecological knowledge and ecofeminism (see Chapter 6, this volume). Indigenous peoples and climate scientists agree that the earth is alive, and that its health is currently suffering. Healthy reconnection to one another and to the earth can help us all heal.

Guiding Principles

Premised on the chapters of this book, these guiding principles highlight the importance of natural landscapes to human and planetary health:

1. Humans modify landscapes, or our surroundings, and there is a reciprocal influence between human health and landscape health.
2. Worldviews are not fixed and are influential in the ways societies interact with landscapes. Current dominant worldviews represent a small sliver of history; we can make other choices.
3. Human-induced environmental devastation negatively influences well-being, especially among the most disenfranchised. Attending to relationships and reciprocity as well as feelings of loss and grief are part of the solution.
4. Healthy intact landscapes can promote well-being through restorative, preventive, and therapeutic mechanisms.
5. An extensive body of research exists, but further research and systematic investigation is needed to more fully understand the effects of interactions between humans and their landscapes.

6. Intentional practices and programs through education, recreation, socialization, and lifestyle can help us develop healthy relationships with our landscapes. Ancient beneficial practices can be recovered and relearned.

7. Intentional design choices can enhance the places where we live and work—promoting the health benefits of nature in urban areas also supports human well-being.

8. We must act quickly. Now is the time.

What Can We Do?

We live in a world that forces us to face many competing interests and make difficult decisions regarding our personal lives, those of our family and friends, and those of our communities and society. A major factor that increases the difficulty of many of these decisions is uncertainty, which forces us to make assumptions based on probabilities. For example, we may earnestly believe that natural landscapes provide us with a great deal of health benefits. A large body of Indigenous knowledge and Western research, as presented in this book, supports that contention. While scientific and research-related questions remain, many scholars agree that "we know enough to act" (Frumkin and Louv, 2007).

If we believe that natural landscapes are beneficial to our health, there are a number of steps we can take to advocate for and protect them:

1. Consider your own relationship with the natural world and continue to develop a sense of personal connection through experiences in natural landscapes.

2. Persuade those around you of the value of natural landscapes in facilitating personal and group health.

3. Build and develop public support for natural landscapes through individual modeling, media, political persuasion, and non-government organization involvement.

4. Help convince the medical profession to prescribe visits to natural landscapes as an acceptable treatment regime. Take a park, not a pill!

5. Learn about local issues related to land protection and management and find ways to get involved.

6. Develop ways to expand learning opportunities regarding the natural world across the educational spectrum, from preschool to college and beyond.

7. Identify and promote activities that can be done in natural landscapes that specifically benefit human health.

8. Continue to learn the histories of oppression and marginalization of people as they relate to natural landscapes and actively work toward reconciliation.

9. Question engrained worldviews and ways of doing things; consider alignment with your desired future.

We envision a future where natural landscapes are recognized for the essential role they play in our collective well-being and are valued, cleaned up, and protected as such. This protection faces a number of obstacles and must operate under a great deal of uncertainty, including a developing scientific base, competing uses of the resource, and barriers to participation such as available time and income, transportation, and a supportive social environment (Yael and Hall, 2020). To be successful, we must educate and listen to the public and pressure the politicians about the value of revitalizing and conserving our natural landscapes, in all of their many forms, for the sake of our individual and collective health.

So, let us move forward with faith in ourselves, in our intelligence, in our indomitable spirit. Let us develop respect for all living things. Let us try to replace violence and intolerance with understanding and compassion. And love.

(Jane Goodall, cited in Redman, 2010, paragraph 10)

References

Alderton, A., Villanueva, K., O'Connor, M., Boulange, C. and Badland, H. (2019) Reducing inequities in early childhood mental health: how might the neighborhood built environment help close the gap? A systematic search and critical review. *International Journal of Environmental Research and Public Health* 16(9): 1516.

American Medical Assocation (AMA) (2020) Racism is a Threat to Public Health. AMA, 16 November. Available at: https://www.ama-assn.org/delivering-care/health-equity/ama-racism-threat-public-health (accessed 23 December 2020).

Cameron, L. and Potvin, C. (2016) Characterizing desired futures of Canadian comunities. *Futures* 82, 37–51. doi: 10.1016/j.futures.2016.05.003.

Centers for Disease Control (2020) About Chronic Diseases. National Center for Chronic Disease Prevention and Health Promotion, US Department of Health & Human Services. Available at: https://www.cdc.gov/chronicdisease/about/index.htm#:~:text=Chronic%20diseases%20such%20as%20heart,in%20annual%20health%20care%20costs (accessed 29 December 2020).

Clark, G.N. and Stankey, G.H. (1979) *The Recreation Opportunity Spectrum: a Framework for Planning, Management, and Research* Vol 98(2). Pacific Northwest Forest and Range Experiment Station, United States Department of Agriculture, Forest Service, Portland, Oregon.

D'Amore, C. and Mitten, D. (2014) Relationship between outdoor experience and body image in female college students. In: Russell, K., Young, A.B. and Boeltz, K.R. (eds) *Coalition for Education in the Outdoors Twelfth Biennial Research Symposium, Bradford Woods, Martinsville, Indiana,* 10–12 January. Coalition for Education in the Outdoors, State University of New York at Cortland, New York, pp. 38–40. Available at: http://www2.cortland.edu/dotAsset/d447c0c5-0bb4-4f4c-a1e7-47a7c4247043.pdf (accessed 29 January 2021).

Degenhardt, B. and Buchecker, M. (2012) Exploring everyday self-regulation in nearby nature: determinants, patterns, and a framework of nearby outdoor recreation behavior. *Leisure Sciences* 34(5), 450–469.

Donovan, G.H., Butry, D.T., Michael, Y.L., Prestemon, J.P., Liebhold, A.M., *et al.* (2013) The relationship between trees and human health: evidence from the spread of the emerald ash borer. *American Journal of Preventive Medicine* 44(2), 139–145.

Donovan, G., Michael, Y., Gatziolis, D., Mannetje, A. and Douwes, J. (2019) Exposure to the natural environment and rurality is protective of ADHD in a large birth cohort of New Zealand children. *Environmental Epidemiology* 3, 103.

Estok, S.C. (2018) *The Ecophobia Hypothesis*. Routledge, Philadelphia, Pennsylvania.

Ewert, A.W., Mitten, D.S. and Overholt, J.R. (2014) *Natural Environments and Human Health*. CAB International, Wallingford, UK.

Frumkin, H. and Louv, R. (2007) The powerful link between conserving land and preserving health. *Land Trust Alliance Special Anniversary Report 2007*, 1–5. Available at: http://www.bio.utexas.edu/courses/THOC/Readings/Nature-Health.pdf (accessed 29 January 2021).

Gascon, M., Triguero-Mas, M., Martínez, D., Dadvand, P., Rojas-Rueda, D., *et al.* (2016) Residential green spaces and mortality: a systematic review. *Environment International* 86, 60–67.

Hayashi, A. (2002) Finding the voice of Japanese wilderness. *International Journal of Wilderness* 8(2), 34–37.

Hayashi, A., Kanamori, M. and Sakatani, M. (2013) The physical load and the recovery process of mountain-climbing activity at the Northern Japan Alps. *Japanese Journal of Mountain Medicine* 33, 45–50.

Keniger, L.E., Gaston, K.J., Irvine, K.N. and Fuller, R.A. (2013) What are the benefits of interacting with nature? *International Journal of Environmental Research and Public Health* 10(3), 913–935.

Lee, I.M., Shiroma, E.J., Lobelo, F., Puska, P., Blair, S.N., *et al.* (2012) Effect of physical inactivity on major non-communicable diseases worldwide: an analysis of burden of disease and life expectancy. *The Lancet* 380(9838), 219–229.

Leopold, A. (1949) *A Sand County Almanac, and Sketches Here and There.* Oxford University Press, New York.

Maantay, J.A. and Maroko, A.R. (2018) Brownfields to greenfields: environmental justice versus environmental gentrification. *International Journal of Environmental Research and Public Health* 15(10): 2233.

Meredith, G.R., Rakow, D.A., Eldermire, E.R., Madsen, C.G., Shelley, S.P., *et al.* (2020) Minimum time dose in nature to positively impact the mental health of college-aged students, and how to measure it: a scoping review. *Frontiers in Psychology* 10: 2942.

Mitchell, R.J., Richardson, E.A., Shortt, N.K. and Pearce, J.R. (2015) Neighborhood environments and socioeconomic inequalities in mental well-being. *American Journal of Preventive Medicine* 49(1), 80–84.

Mitten, D., Overholt, J.R., Haynes, F.I., D'Amore, C.C. and Ady, J.C. (2016) Hiking: a low-cost, accessible intervention to promote health benefits. *American Journal of Lifestyle Medicine* 12(4), 302–310.

Mygind, L., Kjeldsted, E., Hartmeyer, R., Mygind, E., Bølling, M., *et al.* (2019) Mental, physical and social health benefits of immersive nature-experience for children and adolescents: a systematic review and quality assessment of the evidence. *Health & Place* 58: 102136.

National Academies of Sciences, Engineering, and Medicine (2019) *Continuous Improvement of NASA's Innovation Ecosystem. Proceedings of a Workshop.* The National Academies Press, Washington, DC. Available at: https://doi.org/10.17226/25505 (access 23 December 2020).

Oprah.com (2011) The Powerful Lesson Maya Angelou Taught Oprah. Aired on 19 October. Available at: https://www.oprah.com/oprahs-lifeclass/the-powerful-lesson-maya-angelou-taught-oprah-video (accessed 12 February 2021).

Poudyal, N.C., Hodges, D.G., Bowker, J.M. and Cordell, H.K. (2009) Evaluating natural resource amenities in a human life expectancy production function. *Forest Policy and Economics* 11(4), 253–259.

Prehn-Kristensen, A., Zimmermann, A., Tittmann, L., Lieb, W., Schreiber, S., *et al.* (2018) Reduced microbiome alpha diversity in young patients with ADHD. *PLoS One* 13(7): e0200728.

President's Commission on Americans Outdoors (1985) Executive Order 12529. Filed with the Office of the Federal Register, 10:51 a.m., August 16. Office of the Federal Register, National Archives and Records Administration (NARA), Federal Government of the United States of America.

Redman, M. (2010) Jane Goodall Celebrates 50 Years of Activism. Rabble.ca, 4 November. Available at: https://rabble.ca/books/reviews/2010/11/jane-goodall-celebrates-50-years-activism (accessed 10 February 2021).

Schultz, R., Abbott, T., Yamaguchi, J. and Cairney, S. (2018) Indigenous land management as primary health care: qualitative analysis from the interplay research project in remote Australia. *BMC Health Services Research* 18(1): 960.

Siehl, G.H. (2008) The policy path to the great outdoors: a history of the Outdoor Recreation Review Commissions. *Resources for the Future* 15 October. Available at: https://www.rff.org/publications/working-papers/a-history-of-the-outdoor-recreation-review-commissions/ (accessed 29 January 2021).

Simon, J.C., Marchesi, J.R., Mougel, C. and Selosse, M. (2019) Host–microbiota interactions: from holobiont theory to analysis. *Microbiome* 7(5): 5.

Smith, D.G., Martinelli, R., Besra, G.S., Illarionov, P.A., Szatmari, I., *et al.* (2019) Identification and characterization of a novel anti-inflammatory lipid isolated from *Mycobacterium vaccae*, a soil-derived bacterium with immunoregulatory and stress resilience properties. *Psychopharmacology* 236(5), 1653–1670.

Suárez, M., Barton, D.N., Cimburova, Z., Rusch, G.M., Gómez-Baggethun, E., *et al.* (2020) Environmental justice and outdoor recreation opportunities: a spatially explicit assessment in Oslo metropolitan area, Norway. *Environmental Science & Policy* 108, 133–143.

Taylor, D. (2014) *Toxic Communities: Environmental Racism, Industrial Pollution, and Residential Mobility*. NYU Press, New York.

Wagner, L. (2020) *Environmental justice. The Routledge Handbook to the Political Economy and Governance of the Americas*. Routledge, Philadelphia, Pennsylvania.

Watt, W., Lawton, R. and Fujiwara, D. (2018) *Revaluing Parks and Green Spaces: Measuring their Economic and Wellbeing Value to Individuals*. Fields in Trust, London.

Weaver, J. (2019) Greenness may promote heart health. *Environmental Factor* January. National Institute of Environmental Health Sciences. Available at: https://factor.niehs.nih.gov/2019/1/papers/greenness/index.htm (accessed 29 December 2020).

White, M., Alcock, I., Grellier, J., Wheeler, B., Hartig, T., *et al.* (2019) Spending at least 120 minutes a week in nature is associated with good health and wellbeing. *Scientific Reports* 9(1). doi: 10.1038/s41598-019-44097-3.

World Health Organization (WHO) (2020) The Top 10 Causes of Death. WHO, Fact sheet. Available at: https://www.who.int/en/news-room/fact-sheets/detail/the-Top-10-Causes-of-Death (accessed 29 December 2020).

Yael, R. and Hall, C.M. (2020) The camp not taken: analysis of preferences and barriers among frequent, occasional and non-campers. *Leisure Sciences*. doi: 10.1080/01490400.2020.1731885.

Yamamoto, M. (2016) *Exercise Physiology and Training for Mountaineering and Climbing*. Tokyo Shinbun Publishing, Tokyo.

Yeager, R., Riggs, D.W., DeJarnett, N., Tollerud, D.J., Wilson, J., *et al.* (2018) Association between residential greenness and cardiovascular disease risk. *Journal of the American Heart Association* 7(24): e009117. Available at: https://doi.org/10.1161/JAHA.118.009117 (accessed 23 December 2020).

References for Introductory Chapter Quotations

Preface—Richard Louv, journalist and co-founder of Children & Nature Network; Louv, R. (2011) *The Nature Principle: Human Restoration and the End of Nature-Deficit Disorder*. Algonquin Books, Chapel Hill, North Carolina, p. 3.

Chapter 1—Joanna Macy, PhD, environmental activist, eco-philosopher, and scholar of systems theory; Macy, J. (1991) *World as Lover, World as Self: a Guide to Living Fully in Turbulent Times*. Parallax Press, Berkeley, California.

Chapter 2—Suzanne Simard, PhD, forest ecologist who furthered theories about mother trees and intra- and interspecies nutrient sharing; cited in Grant, R. (2018) Do trees talk to each other? *Smithsonian Magazine* March. Available at: https://www.smithsonianmag.com/science-nature/the-whispering-trees-180968084/ (accessed 18 January 2021).

Chapter 3—Robin Wall Kimmerer, PhD, botanist, professor, and member of the Citizen Potawatomi Nation; Kimmerer, R.W. (2013) *Braiding Sweetgrass: Indigenous Wisdom, Scientific Knowledge and the Teachings of Plants*. Milkweed Editions, Minneapolis, Minnesota, p. 327.

Chapter 4—Rachel Kaplan, PhD, environmental psychologist and author of attention restoration theory; Kaplan, R. (1983) The role of nature in the urban context. In: Altman, I. and Whorwill, J. (eds) *Behavior and the Natural Environment*. Plenum, New York, pp. 127–161 (quotation on p. 155).

Chapter 5—Val Plumwood, PhD, ecofeminist and environmental philosopher; Plumwood, V. (2009) Nature in the active voice. *Australian Humanities Review* 46, 113–129 (quotation on p. 116).

Chapter 6—Ellen Swallow Richards (1842–1911), environmental chemist and founder of ecology; Swallow, P.C. (2014) *The Remarkable Life and Career of Ellen Swallow Richards: Pioneer in Science and Technology*. Wiley, Hoboken, New Jersey, p. 95.

Chapter 7—Kevin Lynch (1918–1984), author and urban planner; Lynch, K. (1977) *Growing Up in Cities*. MIT Press, Cambridge, Massachusetts, p. 57.

Chapter 8—Winona LaDuke, environmentalist, political activist, and enrolled with the Ojibwe Nation; LaDuke, W. (1999) *All Our Relations: Native Struggles for Land and Life*. South End Press, Boston, Massachusetts, p. 12.

Index

Note: The page preferences in italics and bold represents figures and tables respectively.

HBD
R+k

Adhya
A-4631

£ 27-50